URBAN LAND POLICY

The Author

Dr. A. Ravindra is an I.A.S. officer with a doctorate in development studies. He has held several important positions including those of Secretary, Housing & Urban Development Department, Karnataka and Commissioner, Bangalore City Corporation. He has also authored a Research Report on "Metropolitan Bangalore: A Management Perspective" and Papers on "Bangalore's Environment Profile" and "Land Transfers in India". His works including the present one reflect both his rich administrative experience and academic scholarship. Presently he is working as Managing Director, Karnataka Power Corporation.

URBAN LAND POLICY

A Metropolitan Perspective

A. RAVINDRA

Indian Administrative Service

CONCEPT PUBLISHING COMPANY, NEW DELHI-110059

ISBN 81-7022-565-5

First Published 1996

Published and Printed by
Ashok Kumar Mittal
Concept Publishing Company
A/15-16, Commercial Block, Mohan Garden
New Delhi-110059
Phones : 5554042, 5504042

PREFACE

Urbanisation is one of the most striking features of modern times. In India, as in most other developing countries, urban population has been growing at a rapid rate and from a figure of 217 million in 1991, it is expected to reach about 300 million by the turn of the century.

The basic infrastructure for development is land. Unfortunately, the importance of proper land management has not been fully realised. In the course of my work in the urban sector, I found land problems most formidable but no clear solutions were forthcoming. The problem is compounded by the absence of a policy framework for promoting orderly urban development in general and land use in particular. This book is an effort in the direction of evolving a suitable Urban Land Policy in India. While I have chosen Bangalore metropolis for detailed study, in view of my familiarity with the city, the issue raised here reflect the problems of Urban India in general and the findings can be relevant to any metropolitan city in the developing world.

The data used in this book are based on 1981 census figures, as the census figures of 1991 were still not available when the study was undertaken. The most significant development in the first half of this decade (nineties) in India has been the ushering in of economic liberalisation. The impact of liberalisation policies are certainly felt more intensely in urban areas. As the demand for urban land increases, the need to treat land as an important resource and ensure its proper management has become all the more relevant. This is perhaps the first comprehensive study on Urban Land Policy covering different aspects like land use planning, land acquisition, land values, land taxation, etc., in a metropolitan perspective. I hope it will be of some use to planners and practitioners and will spur further research in this area.

I would like to thank all those who helped me in bringing out this book, especially Dr. V.K. Tewari, Professor, Indian Institute of Management, Bangalore.

Bangalore **A. Ravindra**
Dated : June 2, 1995

CONTENTS

LIST OF FIGURES

LIST OF TABLES

List of Tables

1

INTRODUCTION

THE URBAN LAND PROBLEM

Land is one of the natural resources of a nation and serves as the basis for human settlements. The rapid growth in population and the process of urbanisation have resulted in an increasing demand for land in urban settlements. A city grows not only by population but by changes in spatial dimensions. The patterns of city growth and its spatial structure are determined by various historical, economic, social and ecological forces that influence urban land use. Land use forms the basis of city structure and exerts a vital influence on the pattern of intra-city development. Proper planning of urban land uses is, therefore, most essential for an orderly and efficent growth of urban areas. "The use of urban land poses serious problems in all countries simply because the supply of surplus land is limited and subject to many competing claims. Dissatisfaction with the emerging urban forms is almost universal. But in the developing countries, where towns and cities often double in area as well as population within a decade, these land problems are most critical." (World Bank, 1983)

The urban population in India has been growing at a much faster rate than the rural population. Between 1971 and 1981, the population in the urban areas increased by 46 per cent compared to 19 per cent in the rural areas. The level of urbanisation in the country in 1981 was 23.7 per cent with a total urban population of about 160 million. The assive concentration of population in urban areas has resulted in serious shortages in housing, water supply and other amenities, growth of slums and spiralling land values. Planning, so far, has lacked a regional dimension, although the Five Year Plans have been advocating balanced development of different regions in the country.

At the root of many of the urban problems, particularly in metropolitan cities, is land. The quantity of land being limited, the pressure on land is increasing as the requirements of civilised life keep growing — for housing, for educational institutions, for office and commercial activities, for industries, for parks and playgrounds; in short, for all the basic requirements of life as well as for socio-economic development. The per capita availability of land in India declined from 3.42 acres in 1901 to 1.18 acres in 1981. The cities are getting more and more congested with rising densities of population. Densities in individual areas in major cities (4,00,000 per sq. km. in Old Delhi and 8,70,000 in Bombay) have reached alarmingly high levels.

The problem of shortage of land is accentuated by the rising land prices in almost all cities. The UN Habitat Conference of 1976 identified sharply rising urban land prices as the most serious of the many problems facing the developing countries in the urbanisation process. The unrealistically high land values have, on the one hand, deprived the ordinary man and particularly the poorer sections, of the ability to pay for the land, and on the other, pushed up the cost of providing urban services to the people. This phenomenon has resulted in a situation of the most desirable space being utilised by powerful social groups. The inability of the poor to find adequate shelter, the uncertainties of tenure, the proliferation of slums, the legal complexities of land rights, the transition of land use from rural to urban — all these raise questions which are crucial to the planning and management of urban growth in India.

Such complex problems of the urban land market inevitably require Government's intervention. Such interventions are devised on the basis of a set of measures aiming to achieve the goals formulated by public authorities. These goals and measures are usually termed as urban land policy. The basic goal of an urban land policy is to achieve optimal utilization of land within the socio-economic objectives of the overall urban development policy.

Any public policy must formulate objectives and describe the instruments through which those objectives are to be achieved. As diverse factors — geographical, social, economic, legal — affect land use, land policies are expected to achieve a variety of objectives. The objectives can be summed up as follows :

(i) an appropriate supply of urban land for community as well as productive activities;
(ii) harmonious urban spatial patterns that minimize the use of resources relative to economic and social benefits;
(iii) greater equity in wealth and income, including access by low income families to adequate shelter;

(iv) a spatial distribution of population and activities at regional and national levels consistent with general national priorities. (World Bank, 1983)

The State has intervened in a number of ways in the urban land market in order to secure an efficient allocation of land and to control the land prices. Basically, State intervention has taken three different yet related forms :

— by legally restricting private rights to use urban land in certain ways (legal measures);
— by the application of a variety of fiscal devices (fiscal measures);
— by directly undertaking acquisition of land and urban development programmes (direct intervention).

Legal restrictions are placed on the use of land by adopting land use planning. The most common instrument employed in this regard is the master plan which allocates land for different uses. Other land use control measures are subdivision regulations and building regulations. Fiscal measures include property tax, tax on vacant land and controls on the pricing of urban goods and services like rent control. These devices may be employed to mop up the surplus value of the land and also as a source of generating revenues. The most important and most common method of direct action by Government is public acquisition of private land and supplying the same for various public purposes like roads, building, transport, public housing etc. Land development and disposal is one of the major tools used not only for augmenting the supply of developed land but also to bring about equity in the distribution of land.

NEED FOR THE STUDY

The shortage of developed land in urban areas and the problems posed by increasing demand on its use by many competing activities require systematic planning and management of urban land within the framework of a well defined urban land policy. Such a policy should be based on a careful analysis of the various forces that influence the use of land by different activity systems in urban areas.

Although extensive studies have been done on the subject of urbanisation and urban development in general, the policy aspects of urban land have not been sufficiently examined. As the World Bank aptly puts it, "the subject is poor in accepted theory and rich in controversy." The main reason for such a state appears to be that the urban land problems are inherently complex and do not lend themselves to easy understanding and analysis.

In India, the first attempt to study the urban land problems was made by the Committee on Urban Land Policy constituted by the Government of India. The Report of this Committee (Government of India, 1965) contains a lucid analysis of the urban land problems and recommendations to overcome them. At the international level, the United Nations and the World Bank have made efforts to deal comprehensively with the subject. *Urban Land Policies and Land Use Control Measures* (UN 1973) deals with particular reference to specific countries including Asian countries. The World Bank brought out two staff working papers on urban land policy issues and opportunities in 1978 and published them in the form of a book in 1983 (World Bank, 1978, and Dunkerley, 1983). This book contains an analysis of the different issues relating to urban land, *viz.*, value of the land, land tenures and instruments through which Government intervention takes place. The Task Force on Housing and Urban Development in its report on "Planning of Urban Development" (Planning Commission, 1983) also examined the issues in Urban Land Policy in India with special reference to the experience of Delhi Development Authority.

The literature on the subject of urban land policy is limited mostly to studies on certain issues like land use, land acquisition, land ceiling, etc., as would be evident from the following: "Land Use Patterns of India's Cities and Towns" (Town and Country Planning Organisation, 1968), "The Theory and Practice of Large Scale Land Development" (Archer, 1974), "Delhi's Large Scale Land Acquisition Development and Disposal Policy: An Appraisal" (Howland, 1975), "Land Use Planning" (Paterson, 1979), "Urban Land Policies: Focus on Land for Housing the Poor" (Naiker, 1983), "Theory and Practice of Urban Land Values in India" (Dange, 1983), "Land Policy and Urban Poor (Buch, 1984), "Urban Land Development Strategy" (Mitra, 1984). A comprehensive analysis of the contents of policy statements laid down from time to time, the measures adopted to implement the policies and their effects on the urban land market in a total perspective of the operation of urban land policy in the Indian context has not been made. This research effort is an attempt in this direction.

Objectives of the Study

The main objective of this study is to critically examine the different components of Urban Land Policy and analyse its implementation with reference to a metropolitan city in India, *viz.*, Bangalore. The specific objectives of the study are the following :

(i) to identify the public policy measures related to urban land matters;
(ii) to analyse the spatial and temporal patterns of urban land values in Bangalore;
(iii) to examine the implementation of urban land policy in Bangalore through instruments of land use planning, fiscal measures, land acquisition and distribution; and
(iv) to suggest guidelines for the formulation of an integrated urban land policy :

Study Area

Bangalore Metropolitan Area constitutes the study area for the purposes of this research. Bangalore has emerged as one of the leading metropolitan cities of India and reflects the various facets of the urban land problem that a growing city faces. Bangalore has been expanding rapidly in size and population. Free from natural barriers, the city is capable of expansion on all sides and attracts migrants from different parts of India. The decade 1971-81 witnessed a population growth rate of 76 per cent, the highest for any metropolitan city in the country. With a population of nearly 3 million in 1981, Bangalore became the fifth largest city in India.

The demand for additional land in Bangalore is reflected in the high urban land values in the city. The land prices in one of the localities in the city have zoomed by over 4,000 per cent during the last 35 years. The government and the public authorities have initiated several measures to deal with urban land problems in Bangalore. Master plans have been prepared, planning and development authorities have been constituted and land has been acquired and distributed for purposes of housing and industry. In spite of these measures, there has been haphazard growth of the city and serious difficulties have been ancountered in meeting the growing needs of the population. Hence, Bangalore serves as a good study area to analyse the urban land policy measures adopted in India.

Scope of the Study

The focus of this study is the operation of urban land policy with reference to a metropolitan city in India, *viz.*, Bangalore. The introductory chapter describes the land problem and the need for State intervention through policy measures. Thereafter the theoretical concepts relevant to an understanding of urban land policy, *viz.*, the theories relating to urban land use, urban land values and urban land use planning as also the spatial framework for land use analysis have been discussed.

The study then deals with urban land policy in India. After identifying the sources and objectives of land policy, the instruments employed to achieve these objectives—by restricting private rights over the use of land and by direct intervention in the land market and their effectiveness have been critically analysed. Before going into the details of the urban land issues pertaining to Bangalore, a background of the study area is provided which includes the geography of the region, urban expansion, demographic features and occupational structure. The regional primacy of Bangalore and its growing importance as a metropolitan city in the national context have been emphasised.

The specific issues pertaining to Bangalore are then taken up for detailed study. First, an attempt has been made to analyse the land values to gain an insight into the functioning of the land market in the city. Thereafter, Government intervention through the urban land policy measures *viz.*, land use planning, land acquisition and disposal, and fiscal measures have been dealt with in three separate chapters. Under land use planning, the implementation of development plans and land use control measures like zoning have been examined. Then the measures to augment the supply of land through land acquisition, the problems faced in the process of acquisition and the role of different land acquisition agencies have been discussed. The operation of fiscal instruments employed by Government through taxation on land and property in Bangalore has been examined with reference to their effectiveness in revenue generation and their role in the context of urban land policy. The legal elements of land use planning, land acquisition and taxation have also been discussed and suitable reforms suggested to make them more effective instruments of land policy.

The concluding chapter gives a summary of the major findings of the thesis and contains a discussion on the relevance of the issues raised in this study and the possible future course of action for formulating a more meaningful urban land policy.

DATA SOURCES AND METHODOLOGY

Collection of data for the purpose of urban land studies is an extremely difficult task. While maintenance of urban land records cannot be said to be satisfactory, the problem is aggravated by the difficulties in gaining access to records or data that are available with different authorities in the Bangalore Metropolitan Area.

The methodology adopted in this study is partly descriptive-analytical, partly evaluative and partly statistical. Data were collected both from primary and secondary sources.

To gain an insight into the policy framework, data were collected from the Five Year Plan documents apart from consulting other Government documents dealing with urban land problems like the Reports of the Committee on Urban Land Policy (1965), the Task Force on Housing Policy (1985) and the National Commission on Urbanisation (1988). The objectives of land policy and the instruments of policy as brought out in these documents have been adopted as the framework within which the experience of Bangalore is analysed.

Data relating to the study area of Bangalore were collected from the following sources :

(i) *the census documents*: data relating to area, population and demographic features, migration, density and occupational patterns;

(ii) *the Outline Development Plan and Comprehensive Development Plan*: the details relating to the area and population with reference to the metropolitan area;

(iii) State Government publications like the Gazetteer of Bangalore District.

In order to understand the legal framework within which urban land policy operates, a study of laws or acts passed by the State Legislature or Parliament, was undertaken. On certain crucial legal issues like payment of compensation when private property is acquired, the reports containing judicial decisions were referred to.

Land use planning has been studied primarily with reference to the two Development Plans of Bangalore — ODP and CDP. The land use requirements determined by these plans under various categories like residential, commercial, etc., have been analysed by making a comparative study of the existing and proposed land uses at different points of time. The zoning regulations and building bye-laws have been analysed obtaining data from the BDA, the Bangalore City Corporation and the Revenue Department. Direct observation of the developments in the city helped to gain an understanding of the operation of zoning regulations and buiding bye-laws.

The fiscal measures have been examined by gathering data from original sources *i.e.* Bangalore City Corporation for property tax and vacant land tax, the BDA for betterment levies and the Department of Registration and Stamps for stamp duty and registration charges. The sources for legal provisions relating to taxation, were, the Karnataka Municipal Corporation Act for the purposes of property tax and the Town and Country Planning Act for the betterment fee.

To analyse the urban land values in Bangalore, data were collected from four different sources :

(a) sale statistics relating to registered values of market transactions from the original registration records of the different Sub-Registrars' offices in the City;
(b) the prices at which the BDA sells land to public compiled from the BDA records;
(c) the standard values fixed by the State Government from the notifications issued; and
(d) price estimates available with Real Estate Agents by direct contact with the Agents.

Field survey was also carried out to know the locational characteristics of different localities chosen for the study and their distance from the city centre. A statistical analysis has been made of the land prices obtaining at different points of time in different localities and for Bangalore City as a whole.

Data relating to land acquisition and disposal were obtained from the concerned authorities—Bangalore Development Authority (BDA), Karnataka Industrial Area Development Board (KIADB) and the Revenue Department of the State Government. The particulars relating to declaration and acquisition under the Urban Land Ceiling Act have been obtained directly from the Government departments concerned. Information pertaining to lands granted or leased in the city was gathered from the records of the City Corporation.

The various land policy measures adopted by Government and public authorities have been evaluated for their effectiveness using the data collected for the study.

ORGANISATION OF THE BOOK

The Book has been organised in nine chapters.

Chapter 1 deals with the urban land problem and sets forth the objectives, scope and methodology of the study.

Chapter 2 discusses the theoretical concepts relating to urban land use, urban land values and urban land use planning, providing a conceptual framework for the study.

Chapter 3 provides an overview of the Urban Land Policy in India — the policy objectives and the operation of policy instruments.

Chapter 4 deals with the study area, *viz.*, Bangalore. The urban growth of the city in terms of physical and demographic changes and the emerging trends of development have been brought out.

Chapter 5 on urban land values contains an analysis of the land price trends in different localities of the city.

Chapter 6 deals with land use planning in Bangalore. The planning process and the measures of land use control in force in the city have been analysed.

Land acquisition and disposal and the role of different agencies in the supply of land for various purposes have been discussed in Chapter 7.

Chapter 8 examines the fiscal policies. Different taxes levied in respect of urban land in Bangalore have been discussed.

The last chapter, *i.e.* Chapter 9 gives the major conclusions of the study and puts forward suggestions for the formulation of an integrated urban land policy.

2

URBAN LAND POLICY : THEORETICAL CONCEPTS

THEORIES OF URBAN LAND USE

Urban land use has been studied by scholars of different disciplines from their respective angles. Geographers, sociologists, economists and town planners have analysed this problem in the social as well as a spatial context. These studies have shown that similar land uses and population groups tend to cluster at various locations within a city. Actual locations of the land uses are determined by a complex combination of social, economic and administrative factors. Some of these studies have resulted in formulation of theories of urban land use patterns, land values and land use planning. These are presented in the following sections :

ECOLOGICAL APPROACH

The starting point for considering the concepts relating to the utilisation of land in cities is the theory propounded by Burgess (1925) according to which urban land use tended to display a zonal organisation. He recognises five concentric zones—the central business district, zone of transition, zone of workingmen's homes, zone of better residence and the commuters' zone. This model was perceived by Burgess as an ideal construction of the tendencies of any town or city to expand concentrically from its central business district. The down-town area is normally encircled by an area of transition which is being invaded by business and light manufacturing activities. The third zone is inhabited by the workers in industries who have escaped the area of deterioration but who desire to live within easy access of their work. Beyond this zone is the residential area of high class apartment buildings. Still further out, beyond the city limits, is the commuters' zone — sub-urban area of satellite cities.

Burgess's model was derived from the observation of American cities in general, and Chicago in particular, and constituted the spatial expression of the ecological principles of competition, segregation, dominance, invasion and succession. The model has often been criticised as too generalised and unrealistic in the context of modern cities (Gittus, 1964). Its emphasis on clearcut boundaries has been seen as arbitrary. According to the critics of this model, Burgess was "drawing lines that don't exist around areas that don't matter" (Kimble, 1951). The model is also considered too limited historically and culturally to enable a clear understanding of land use patterns of modern metropolitan cities. However, this pioneering effort provided a generalised view of organisation of land uses in urban areas, based on certain well articulated principles of urban spatial process.

Hoyt (1939) who put forth the 'sector theory' examined the residential rent patterns in 25 cities in USA and concluded that the residential areas of different rent levels in American cities tended to conform to a pattern of sectors rather than of concentric circles. He was primarily concerned with residential uses and showed that the location of high status areas determined much of the other land use patterning within the city; they tended to move outward along radial lines in distinct sectors. Therefore, the city structure becomes sectoral in character.

Harris and Ulman (1945) presented the multiple nuclei model according to which cities do not grow simply about a central business district but are formed by the integration of a number of separate nuclei into the urban fabric. These nuclei are not located in relation to any genéralised zone but in accordance with the pattern of activities. Some activities group together—like theatre lands for instance, as they stand to benefit from association, while some other activities repel each other - like separation of higher quality houses from industry. Harris and Ulman argued that during the process of the growth of cities, these influences would condition the emergence of separate areas, which would be neither zones nor sectors but 'patches' joined together.

The classical ecological approach looked upon urban land as subject to competition from rival interests carried on at a 'sub-social' level. "Ecological interaction underlines many aspects of community life" says Quinn (1939) and argues that "merchants who want strategic commercial sites at the heart of the city compete for the limited supply of land in this location" and urban residents "bid for the limited supply of residential space". This line of economic determination was objected to by Firey (1945) who contended that culturally rooted values exert a 'causative' influence on urban land use patterns. He felt that areas often get symbolic connotations and hence cannot be explained in an economic analysis.

Traditional burial grounds and churches may be preserved in the central area and prosperous ethnic minorities may continue to reside in slums.

Form (1954) argued in favour of discarding the idea of a free unorganised market in which individuals compete impersonally. It would then be necessary to identify who are the largest consumers of land, which organisations deal in land, and which associations mediate conflicts of land use. Four organisational complexes play a dominant role : the real estate and building business; larger industries, businesses and utilities; individual home owners, and local government agencies. The role of each of them would depend on the functions it performs in terms of the land use market and the resources or influence it can deploy.

There were also attempts to enumerate the variables which influence land use in order to define an 'ecological complex'—like environment, technology, population and organisation (Schnore, 1965); site, accessibility, growth and persistence (Duncan, 1964).

Activity Systems Approach

In a broad sense, land use is concerned with human activity. Activity systems deal with behaviour patterns of individuals, institutions and firms which occur in spatial patterns. Advocated by Chapin (1965), this approach provides "a conceptual framework to describe some of the major elements and dynamics of human behaviour as they relate to land use." Values held by individuals or groups with respect to the use of a particular area set in motion a four phase cycle of human behaviour, *viz.*, experiencing needs and wants; defining goals; planning alternatives; deciding and acting. The behaviour patterns are seen as constituting systems of activity which may be classified as routine activities, institutionalized activities, and organisation of processes. For instance, a well defined legal area may emerge in a city as a result of a system of activities and linkages which bind legal firms together. It, therefore, becomes necessary to identify the systems and linkages of an activity to gain a proper understanding of the pattern of land use. The 'activity systems' concept attempts to first examine the city in micro-detail and then builds up a framework for the total structure using the 'systems approach'

THEORIES OF URBAN LAND VALUES

The concept of land value may be described as "the monetary evaluation of land use. It is dependent upon both the present and future use which, in turn, is influenced by the physical and economic characteristics of the site and the social control of land use" (Clarke, 1965). According to Lichfield (1956), values are created and changed by the same forces that create and change uses. Clarke has clarified that the value may also change before any change of use actually takes place. *For example*, where the site possesses value for a future use its potential is reflected in the present price or rent. Value may, therefore, be classified as "current value", *i.e.*, value for the present use or "potential value", *i. e.*, value for a different and usually more valuable use at some future date.

Land value can be considered in two contexts. One is the market value, which is the price of a land parcel negotiated at the time of sale of the parcel, and the other is the assessed value, which is the estimated worth of the parcel made by a competent private or public assessor (Northam, 1975). The market value of a piece of land may be different from the assessed value.

The first important work on urban land values was written by R. M. Hurd (1901), often regarded as the father of modern land economics. He adopted the principles put forward by Ricardo for agricultural land to the urban field: "Value in urban land, as in agricultural land, is the resultant of economic or ground rent capitalized." Nevertheless, his work recognized the importance of land use: "the patterns of land uses and land values will be mutually determining." He emphasised the role of competitive bidding for land in determining urban land uses and the influence of accessibility on land values. He summed up his work thus: "Since value depends on economic rent and rent on location and location on convenience and convenience on nearness, we may eliminate the intermediate steps and say that value depends on nearness" (Hurd, 1924). However, Hurd recognized that 'nearness' is a relative term and factors like physical structures (height of building, layout etc.) and the nature of use must be taken into account.

Alfred Marshall (1916) introduced the concept of 'location value', which is expressed in the financial advantage derived from the location of the site. According to him, the site value was equal to the agricultural rental and the location value. In other words, the urban land value is determined by adding the location factor to the agricultural land value. One other factor influencing the value of urban land is the amount of floor space in a building.

R. M. Haig (1926) introduced the notion of the 'friction of space', *i.e.*, hindrance to perfect or immediate accessibility, for without such 'friction' there would be no transport costs and all locations would be perfect. He tried to establish a three-way relation of rent, transport costs and location which is interdependent. Rent constituted the charge for accessibility or the saving in transport cost while the occupancy and use of land is determined by a bidding process.

Ratcliff (1949), carrying forward the argument of Haig opined that the utilization of land was ultimately determined by the relative efficiencies of the uses in various locations. Efficiency in use is measured by the ability to pay rent and the use that can extract the greatest return from a given site will be the successful bidder. And, from all this emerges an "orderly pattern of land use spatially organised to perform most efficiently the economic functions that characterize urban life."

The theories of Hurd and Ratcliff are based on certain assumptions — for instance, all users are assumed to require equal quantities of land, which are not proven. Factors like substitution of a large piece of land for a less convenient location or buying cheaper land in a distant location are not taken into account. A more detailed model was presented by William Alonso (1964) who introduced two further variables—the quantity of land which each user would wish to acquire and the amount of disposable income which will be devoted to land and travel costs on the one hand, and all goods and services, including savings on the other. "The price of land . . . . decreases with increasing distance from the centre. Therefore, the quantity of land that may be bought increases with the distance, since land is becoming cheaper. On the other hand, distance enters . . . . in the form of commuting costs. As distance increases, so do commuting costs and consequently the amount of land that may be purchased decreases." The formulation is like an individual equilibrium solution, a pattern of preferences set against different contributions of land, goods and accessibility. This model is again based on assumptions such as all land of equal quality, land ready for use without improvement, land freely bought and sold without legal or planning restraints.

Northam (1975) developed a theory of urban land values based on the concept of 'bid-rent', meaning the amount of capital one is willing to bid or offer for use of a specified land parcel. In the case of urban land, different land users have different abilities to pay. The rent paying ability of users depends on a number of factors like the size of the city, the specific use to which the land parcel would be put, individual preferences and the land stock available in a particular city. Northam (1975) has shown that the bid rent curve for commercial users of land reaches the greatest level (**Fig. 2.1**). This level would be greatest at the point of greatest desirability, coinciding with the point of maximum value. The willingness to buy

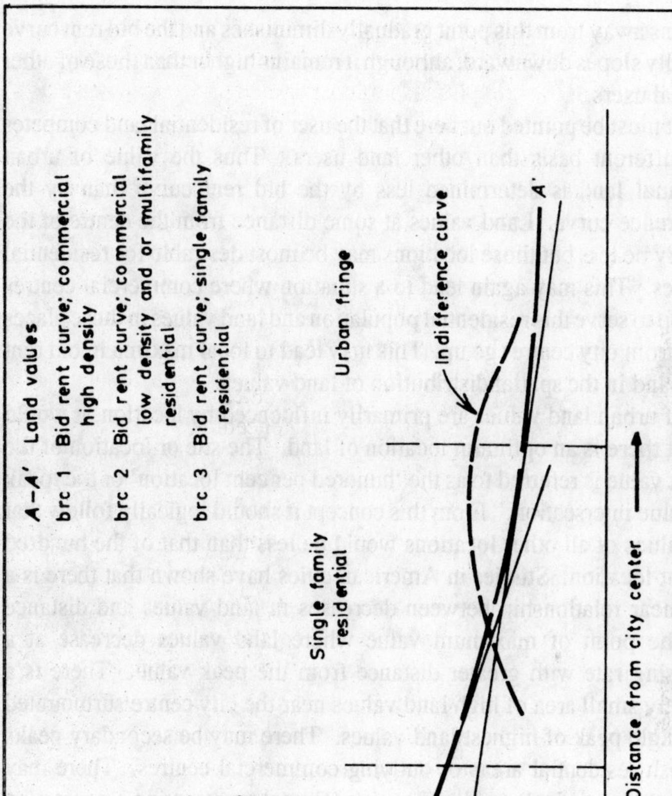

SOURCE: Northam R M (1975), Urban Geography, John Wiley and Sons, New York

Fig. 2.1 : Bid rent curves for selected urban land uses and the indifference curve

locations away from this point gradually diminishes and the bid rent curve gradually slopes downward, although it remains higher than those of other potential users.

It must be pointed out here that the user of residential land competes on a different basis than other land users. Thus the value of urban residential land is determined less by the bid rent curve than by the indifference curve. Land values at some distance from the centre of the city may be less but those locations may be most desirable for residential purposes. This may again lead to a situation where commercial centres come up to serve this residential population and land values in these places (away from city centre) go up. This may lead to local maxima in bid rent curves and in the spatial distribution of land values.

If urban land values are primarily influenced by location, it would suggest there is an optimum location of land. The site or location of the highest value is referred to as the 'hundred per cent location' or the 'peak land value intersection.' From this concept it should logically follow that land values of all other locations would be less than that of the hundred per cent location. Studies in American cities have shown that there is a curvilinear relationship between decreases in land values and distance from the point of maximum value where land values decrease at a decreasing rate with greater distance from the peak value. There is a relatively small area of high land values near the city centre surmounted by a single peak of highest land values. There may be secondary peaks like posh residential areas or outlying commercial centres. There may also be pockets of substandard housing (slums) representing a depression in the statistical surface.

LAND USE PLANNING CONCEPTS

Urban land use planning is part of the urban planning process which in turn is part of the general planning process. In a broad sense, planning is the allocation of scarce resources to achieve certain goals. Land use planning involves the regulation of land use with the objective of achieving efficient utilisation of land resources.

The planning processes commonly used in urban planning are master planning, comprehensive planning and structure planning. 'Comprehensive planning' and 'master planning' are used synonymously and have a long range perspective of 20 to 30 year. Structure planning highlights the critical issues and establishes priority areas where growth or change should take place. Land use planning constitutes a vital part of the general or comprehensive planning process. Three categories of planning goals can be identified with regard to land use :

(a) planning's main task is to reconcile competing claims for the use of limited land so as to provide a consistent, balanced and orderly arrangement of land use;
(b) planning's central function is to provide a good (or better) physical environment; a physical environment of such good quality is essential for the promotion of a healthy and civilised life;
(c) planning, as part of a broader social programme, is responsible for providing the physical basis for a better community level (Foley, 1960).

Planning Techniques

A number of new concepts and techniques of planning have evolved since the beginning of the century. Ebenezer Howard (1898) propounded the 'Garden City' theory. According to this theory, it is better to construct a New Town on a virgin land than improve or extend an already established Town. In the case of the former, the initial cost of land is cheap and as the price of land increases, the pace of development steps up and the increase in land value can be used for the benefit of the community; in the case of the latter, land values are very high and the cost of land acquisition and development becomes prohibitive. Moreover, the benefits of improvement go more to private owners than to the community. The 'Garden City' is a city complete with housing, industry, educational, recreational and shopping facilities. It is to be constructed as a 'satellite' of a metropolitan town with a density of population not exceeding 30 persons per acre and to be surrounded by an agricultural belt.[1]

Patrick Geddes (1915) emphasised the organic concept of a Town. A town is not an inanimate thing like roads, buildings and gardens but the 'people', a living organism. A town is an integration of 'Folk, Work and Place'. A plan must take into account the number and kind of people living in the town, their needs for work and the place where they live and carry on their activities.[2] Geddes advocated a new technique of planning and called for 'Diagnostic Surveys' of towns. 'Survey before Plan and Plan before Development'. As a town cannot be planned independently without considering its regional setting, Geddes also emphasised the importance of 'Regional Planning.' A Regional Development Plan must actually precede a Town Development Plan. This technique of planning, with suitable changes, is applied in most Western countries.

The first Town Planning Act was enacted in the UK in 1909 with the aim of providing "the home healthy, the house beautiful, the town pleasant, the city dignified and the suburb salubrious." This ideal could not, however, be achieved and the two World Wars generated problems of unbalanced development resulting in congestion in London and the surrounding areas. To study these problems, three Commissions were set up - Barlow, Scott and Uthwatt. Following the recommendations of these commissions—which served as the basis for Town Planning Legislation, a New Town and Country Planning Act was enacted in the UK in 1947. The concept of Town Planning underwent a complete change under this law as country was also included under planning. The Local Planning Authorities were asked to prepare a 'Land Use' Plan for the area under their jurisdiction. This subsequently became the Development Plan which is sanctioned by the government and is implemented by the planning authorities. The Town Planning Legislation and practices in India are based mostly on this British model.

Land Use Plan

'Planning' must be distinguished from 'plan'. The former is a dynamic process with an action—oriented goal; the latter is designed to achieve certain targets within a specified period. 'Land Use Plan' is sometimes confused with 'land use map' or with 'zoning plan'. A land use map is a map showing how the land and structures on it are used for certain purposes at a particular time, whereas, a land use plan is a proposal for the future use of land and the structures built on it. Zoning is a legal device to implement the proposals for land development contained in the land use plan. Broadly, "the land use plan reflects an analysis of urban activity systems and a carefully studied estimate of future land requirements for expansion and renewal, showing how development in the urban area should proceed in the future to insure the best possible physical environment for urban living, the most economic use of land, and the proper balance in use from a cost revenue point of view." (Chapin, Jr. 1965)

A land use plan should generally include the following :

(i) Statement of objectives;

(ii) Description of the existing urban setting and land characteristics;

(iii) Future land requirements — qualitative and quantitative; and
(v) Presentation of plan alternatives — the proposals involved in each of the alternatives and the policy implications are identified.

The land use plan should serve as a guide to develop a comprehensive plan for urban or metropolitan growth and development. Such a plan would include a programme for implementation comprising : (a) regulatory measures like zoning and subdivision control; (b) development measures for public or private action; and (c) public policies relating to tax reform, provision of services etc.

SPATIAL FRAME WORK FOR LAND USE ANALYSIS

Scholars have analysed the complex problem of land use mainly with reference to specific spatial areas such as Central Business District, social areas, industrial areas and the rural-urban fringe. These concepts are discussed below:

Central Business District (CBD)

CBD is considered the centre around which the rest of the city is structured. Murphy and Vance (1954) who attempted to define a CBD began by indicating the non-central uses: permanent residence, government and public buildings, organisational establishments (colleges, churches etc.), industrial establishments, wholesaling, commercial storage, vacant plots and buildings. Thereafter, the central characteristics such as intensive use of space, higher land values, heavier pedestrian traffic and generally taller buildings are identified. In view of the dynamic nature of CBD, its edges keep advancing or contracting. Then emerges the Zone in Transition which according to Preston and Griffin (1966) has been traditionally viewed as an area of mixed commercial and non-commercial land use, and separating the retail heart of the city from surrounding residential neighbourhoods or heavy industrial districts. As more space is demanded by central users, residential uses extend outward. The Zone in Transition, therefore, experiences the greatest change of use. The upward growth of CBD and the development of industry and retail trade in the sub-urban area results in reducing demand for space in areas not experiencing shortage. Consequently, the old building stock deteriorates and in the absence of renewal, there is decay.

Social Areas

Deriving from the analysis of Burgess, it is generally believed that as the city grows outward from the centre, new houses are built on the periphery. But only the richer sections of population can afford new types of houses. As they keep moving outward, concentric residential zones are formed with increasing income and social status, the older outward houses filtering down to lower income groups. It is also argued in structural terms that larger the city, greater is the distance to be traversed to the central areas and as such the upper classes may also be found in luxury apartments near the city centre.

According to the hypotheses dealing with social characteristics, populations are segregated residentially by social class. Using occupation as a measure of social class, Duncan and Duncan (1955) concluded that "residential segregation is greater for those occupational groups with clearly defined status than for those groups whose status is ambiguous." They found an essential correspondence of social and spatial distance among occupational groups. Studies by Duncans and others like Wheeler (1986), Shevky and Bell (1955) and Johnson (1966) bring out two major factors which affect the decision : where to live in a city, *viz.*, socio-economic status and life-cycle 'status' where the family's needs exercise a strong influence. Shevky isolated a third component, *viz.*, ethnic status. According to Morioty (1970), residential choice is guided by two competing hypotheses. The first is 'economic competition' where the ability to pay becomes the basic factor and journey to work and site act as major influences. The second is 'social choice' according to which values, needs and desires of people play a vital role. Other studies have attempted to list desirable qualities like better neighbourhood, access to good schools, modern architectural style etc. [Butler (1960), Petersen (1967) Chapin (1969) etc].

Industrial Areas

Scholars like Lowenstein (1963), Prod (1964) and Hamilton (1967) tried to develop models of industrial location in which the following types are identified :

(i) Centrally located : (a) labour oriented, (b) market oriented, and (*c*) CBD oriented;

(ii) Non-local market high value industries : These tend to have random locations;

(iii) Large basic processing industries: Although sub-urban locations are ideal since the problems caused by noise and pollution can be minimised, many of these especially chemical and metallurgical industries are found in the older inner areas of cities;
(iv) Water front or port industries;
(v) Integrated industries along communication lines: These would include non-centrally located 'communications-economy' industries; and
(vi) Sub-urban industries: the product of the process of decentralization.

The above types and locations bring out the fact that industry can be found in every zone of a city from the CBD to the suburb. A proper understanding of the industrial land use pattern can be gained by studies of the locational behaviour of individual firms.

The Rural-Urban Fringe

The growth of a city outward does not usually take place in a well defined and planned way. The space into which the city extends in the process of its growth had led to the concept of rural-urban fringe. In an attempt to define this fringe area, Golledge (1960) termed it an area of 'great differentiation'. The area, partly rural and partly being brought into the urban fold is characterised by variety of land uses. The following features broadly characterised any rural-urban fringe :

(i) There is a constantly changing pattern of land occupance;
(ii) Farms are small;
(iii) Crop production is intensive;
(iv) The provision of services and public utilities is incomplete; and
(v) Speculative building activity is common.

Another view advocated by Paul (1965) related the concept of the fringe to social processes as distinct from the physical area. He pointed out that a new population is invading local communities, bringing in national values and class consciousness at the same time that a new type of community, associated with dispersed living is emerging.

As the urban frontier extends into the rural area, several problems relating to land use arise. Two important problem areas in the rural-urban fringe identified by Mayer (1967) relate to competition for land and preservation of open space.

CONCLUSION

In conclusion, it may be stated that urban land problems are complex and there is no coherent thought or structure of principles which can easily help in formulation of land policy. Even the broad area of urban planning bristles with difficulties when it comes to the question of formulating a valid theory. ". . . . very little comprehensive City Planning Theory is well enough established to apply in practice" (Branch, 1975). The study of urban land policy has, therefore, to be undertaken by identifying the elements that contribute to such a policy, *viz.*, land use, land values, and Land Use Planning. Although different theories may be employed to explain each of these elements, it must be recognized that they are inter-related. The use to which land is put and proposed to be put influences the value of the land. The land market is influenced by both the use and value of the land. The operation of these forces in turn influences the Planning of Land Use and Development.

In the context of Indian cities, the unplanned development in the periphery has raid the question of limiting the size of cities and preventing the expanding urban sprawl. At the same time planning has to face the issue of providing adequate space to meet the needs of the growing population. Policy decisions are crucial in resolving this dichotomy. Hence, the need for evolving a meaningful Urban Land Policy.

NOTES

1. The idea of Howard put-forth in his influential work 'Tomorrow: A Peaceful Path to Social Reform' (1886) received great acclaim and in 1902 a garden city, Lechworth, was started about 56 km from London. This was followed up by another garden city, Welwyn, in 1920.
2. In his work "Cities in Evolution" (1915), Geddes coined the term 'connurbation' to describe the waves of population inflow to large cities, followed by overcrowding and slum formation, and then wave of backflow — the whole process resulting in amorphous sprawl, waste, and unnecessary absolescence.

3

URBAN LAND POLICY IN INDIA

Land reform measures were initiated in rural India soon after indepedence in 1947. Various states passed legislations aimed at re-structuring land tenure systems. Urban Land Reforms were, however, slow in coming. There were some announcements on policy and legislative enactments pertaining to Town Planning in the 'fifties' and 'sixties'. Some public interventions in different forms were also made in the land market. But the first major step aimed at fundamental reforms in the Urban Land Systems came only in 1976 when a comprehensive land ceiling legislation took shape.

Despite these efforts, India lacks a comprehensive Urban Land Policy. Neither the Government of India nor the State Government has formulated any such policy. While one may find expressions of intention and isolated policy announcements, there has been no consistent 'Urban Land Policy' formulated on the basis of a detailed study of the problems that will be encountered or of the policy instruments available for dealing with these problems (Acharya, 1988). An attempt has been made in this chapter to povide an overview of the Urban Land Policy issues in India and the efforts made by government through different policy instruments to deal with these issues.

SOURCES OF LAND POLICY

The following constitute the vital sources of urban policy matters in India :

(i) Reports/papers brought out by the Central or State Government.
(ii) Five Year Plans,
(iii) Legislation.

Government Reports and Papers

(i) *Report of the Committee on Urban Land Policy* : The first attempt towards evolving an Urban Land Policy was made when the Government of India (Ministry of Health) constituted a Committee to examine the problems relating to Urban Land Policy in 1963. The report submitted by the Committee in 1965 must be considered as a landmark in the field of Urban Policy Literature in India. The Committee took note of the declining man-land ratio and considering a comprehensive long-range policy imperative, suggested a package of Urban Land Policy measures.

(ii) *Task Force on Housing and Urban Development* : The Planning Commission set up Task Forces to evolve a long term perspective on housing and Urban Development Issues in 1982. The Task Force on 'Planning of Urban Development' which submitted its report in 1983 critically examined, *inter alia*, the problems of Urban Land Policies in India. It reviewed the existing approaches to land policy, especially with reference to Delhi and called for a new approach to promote efficiency in the allocation of land and to help the poor in their access to land for shelter.

(iii) *National Housing Policy* : The National Housing Policy document of the Government of India (1988) emphasised the need for the formulation and implementation of a purposeful land policy in the context of achieving the goal of eradicating houselessness in the country by the turn of the century. It also suggested strategies to augment the supply of land, particularly to meet the housing requirements of the weaker sections.

(iv) *National Commission on Urbanisation (1988)* : An important step towards understanding the urban problems of the country was taken by the Government of India when it appointed National Commission on Urbanisation. The Commission in its Report examined the dimensions of urbanisation and the issues relating to the existing urban patterns and policies in India and made recommendations on the range of policy interventions necessary to bring about 'more human and efficient urban settlements.' It identified the failure to anticipate the rising demand for urban land and ensure an adequate supply of land at affordable prices as 'possibly the most disastrous feature of the past four decades of urbanisation in India'. Emphasising the significance of urbanised land as a vital resource that needs to be generated in sufficient quantities for appropriate uses, the commission strongly advocated a realistic land policy to overcome the problems of shortage of urban land and the rising land prices.

(v) *Background paper on Urban Policy in Karnataka*: This document presented by the Housing and Urban Development Department of Karnataka to the Economic and Planning Council of the State in 1984 examined the urban problems of the State including those of Bangalore and suggested measures to tackle among others, problems relating to land and housing in Bangalore City.

Five Year Plans

The Five Year Plans constitute an important source of State policy on issues relating to Socio-economic Development in India. While the first two plans of the Central Government recognised the need for formulation of policies relating to Urban Planning and Development, the first serious effort at laying down a broad policy with regard to urban development was made while formulating the Third Five Year Plan. The Plan referred to the high costs of urban development in rapidly growing urban areas and proposed measures to control urban land values. The Fourth Five Year Plan stressed the need for an Urban Land Policy and called for action on the recommendations of the Report of the Committee on Urban Land Policy of 1965.

The Fifth Five Year Plan is of great significance so far as Urban Land Policy is concerned. It recognised that 'perhaps the most important instrument necessary for achieving a breakthrough in urban development will be the formulation of Urban Land Policy.' It described the broad objectives of such a policy and also the tools for the implementation of those objectives. In the Sixth Plan the thrust of urbanisation policy was on development of small and medium towns and achieving balanced distribution of urban population. The Seventh Five Year Plan called for slowing down of the growth of big metropolises and stressed the need for preparation of regional and sub-regional Urban Development Plans.

Legislation

Legislation is a source as well as an instrument of public policy. The State seeks to achieve many of its policy objectives through enactment of laws. A major difficulty in the articulation of urban land policy is the plethora of existing legislation and regulation which govern the land market (Planning Commission, 1983). These laws relate primarily to land use regulation which restrict private rights, and direct intervention in the land market to gain social control of land.

The Constitution of India vests the power to enact laws relating to land with the State Government[2]. Acquisition and requisition of properties, however, is a concurrent power enjoyed both by the Central and State governments[3]. The most important constitutional provision in relation to Urban Land Policy is Article 19(1)(f) which confers on individuals the right to property. The operation of this provision is, however, restricted by Article 19(5) which empowers the State to place reasonable restrictions on property rights in public interest. It is this provision which enables the State to directly acquire private land or restrict private rights over land. The various laws governing the land market passed by the Central and State governments may be classified as follows :

1. Town Planning Legislation including Urban Development Authority Acts—
   to control the use of land with a view to regulate its planned growth and development.
2. Land Acquisition Act—
   to acquire land for public purposes.
3. Municipal enactments including building byelaws—
   to control building activity.
4. Slum Improvement and Clearance Act—
   to improve the living conditions of slum dwellers.
5. Urban Land Ceiling and Regulation Act—
   to impose ceiling limits on land holdings and achieve equitable distribution of urban land.

The laws enacted by the Government of Karnataka which are applicable to Bangalore are given in Table 3.1.

Basically, all these laws contain elements which control or regulate the use of land. Hence, they are also aimed at facilitating the operation of land use policy. While the Reports of Committees and the Five Year Plans have articulated the policy objectives and strategies to achieve them, actual implementation is made possible through the instrumentality of legislation.

TABLE 3.1: **Legislation affecting Urban Land Policy in Karnataka**

Law	*Purpose*
1. (a) The Karnataka Town and Country Planning Act, 1961	To control the use of land with a view to regulate its planned growth and development.
(b) The Bangalore Development Authority Act, 1976.	
(c) The Bangalore Metropolitan Region Development Authority Act, 1985.	
2. (a) The Land Acquisition Act, 1894	To acquire lands for public purposes including industrial development.
(b) The Karnataka Industrial Areas Development Board Act, 1966	
3. (a) Karnataka Municipal Corporation Act, 1976	To control developments of land and building activity.
(b) Zoning Regulations and Building Byelaws	
4. The Karnataka Slum Improvement and Clearance Act, 1973	To improve the living conditions of slum dewellers.
5. The Urban Land Ceiling Act, 1976	To achieve equitable distribution of urban land.
6. Miscellaneous Acts like the Karnataka Land Reforms Act, 1961, Karnataka Land Revenue Act, 1964, Karnataka Rent Control Act, 1962.	Certain provisions of these acts relating to transfer of agricultural land, conversion of agricultural land and determination of fair rent for leased properties can affect Urban Land Policy decisions.

OBJECTIVES OF URBAN LAND POLICY

Any policy relating to land must begin with a statement of objectives. The Committee on Urban Land Policy (1965) outlined four basic objectives, *viz.*, optimum social use of urban land, supply of adequate quantity of land at reasonable prices, encouraging community effort for land development and housing, and preventing concentration of land ownership. It classified land into different categories—developed urban land, undeveloped urban land, land within urbanisable limits, land beyond urbanised limits and the land use of which is frozen, and recommended certain measures to be taken in respect of each category of land. The Task Force on Urban Development (1983), considering the general population pressure on land and the rapid urban growth in the country, added two new objectives to the four mentioned above and restated the objectives of Urban Land Policy in the Indian context as follows :

(i) to achieve an optimum social use of urban land;
(ii) to make land available in adequate quantity, at the right time and at reasonable prices to both the public authorities and the individuals;
(iii) to encourage co-operative community effort and *bona fide* individual builders in the field of land development, housing and construction;
(iv) to widen the base of land ownership specially to safeguard the interest of the poor and under-privileged sections of urban society;
(v) to encourage the socially and economically efficient allocation of urban land such that land development is done in a resource conserving manner and that the magnitude of land used is optimal, and
(vi) to promote flexibility in land use in response to changes resulting from a growing city.

The Five Year Plans reiterated these objectives in one form or the other. Planners and policy makers in India have, by and large, considered control of urban land values and attainment of equity in the distribution of land as major objectives of land policy.

INSTRUMENTS OF URBAN LAND POLICY AND GOVERNMENT INTERVENTION

Although no conscious policy relating to urban land has been formulated, the Central and State governments have adopted a number of measures from time to time aimed at achieving one or the other policy objectives mentioned above. Hence, an assessment of the Urban Land Policy in India can be done only in the context of the measures undertaken so far.

The policy instruments employed to achieve the objectives outlined above are the following :

1. Master Plan including restrictions on land use;
2. Land Acquisition and Disposal;
3. Urban Land Ceiling;
4. Taxation.

While the operational details of these instruments for Bangalore will be discussed separately, a broad assessment of their impact in the national context is attempted below:

Master Plan

The legal sanction for preparation of the Master Plan is derived from the Town and Country Planning Act. The objective of regulating the planned growth of land use and development is sought to be achieved through the instrument of Master Plan or 'Development Plan'. Development Plans have been prepared for a number of cities in India. The Master Plan for Delhi (1962) was the first attempt of preparation of a comprehensive Plan for a Metropolitan City in India. The Calcutta Basic Development Plan was prepared in 1966 and taken up for implementation in 1970. Other major cities also started preparing their own plans. But the degree of enforcement and effectiveness of implementation vary from State to State and from city to city. Broadly, the following comments can be made on the operation of Master Plans and the restrictions placed on land use :

(a) The law provides a very elaborate procedure for the preparation of a Master Plan—from declaration of the intention to prepare a plan to actual preparation of the draft plan, the final plan and accord of sanction by Government. The process usually takes much longer than the prescribed time limit. Planning activity is not matched by implementation to the desired extent. Implementation of development plans in India is said to be 'marginal' and far too slow.

(b) Land Use Planning which is part of the Master Plan is primarily based on population forecasts. The allocation of land for different uses is made with reference to norms such as density, schools or health facilities per unit of population. Such an approach suffers from two shortcomings. First, there is no connection between investment implications of the Master Plan and resource availability, and secondly, the land use allocation exercise and the standards used do not deal adequately with the socio-economic conditions of the people (Planning Commission, 1983).

(c) The Master Plan usually incorporates development control measures which serve as instruments of land use regulation, *viz.*, zoning, subdivision and building regulations. Zoning, which implies demarcation of a city into zones has been criticised as unsuited to Indian conditions. As the concept is based on separation of land uses, it goes against the interests of the poor. When work zone and residential zone are separated, people are forced to commute adding to their cost of living, and necessitating a good transportation system. In developed countries, zoning and location planning are linked to transportation systems. "The Indian City structure is not and cannot be wholly formal and fitted into a neat plan of land use zones" (Buch, 1987). Another disadvantage of zoning is that it can create an uneven distribution of land-value patterns, and this encourages speculative dealing (Archer, 1974).

(d) Building regulations, which prescribe the height of the building, the materials to be used in construction, floor area ratio etc., have, it is argued, acted as impediments to the efficient use of land in growing cities. Where, *for example*, the height of a building is restricted to two or three storeys or large setbacks are to be provided limiting the size of the building, the effect would be to make land scarce even in accessible areas. This results in a decrease in the value of buildings in relation to land values. Low density development leads to an extension of the urban sprawl and extensive rather than intensive development patterns. Land becomes more scarce resulting in speculation and an increase in land values. Overrigidity in design and standards would push up building costs on the one hand, and restrict the supply of housing on the other. In a country like India, very high standards tend to encourage illegal and unauthorised constructions.

(e) The Master Plans have provided a physical frame of land use for a projected city population over a period of 15-25 year. Some of them have also included programmes for urban development—like land development and housing in the case of Delhi, and water supply and transport in the case of Calcutta. But the dominant objective of most such plans has been regulation and enforcement rather than socio-economic development. The instrument of the Master Plan has not proved adequate to fulfil the goal of planning as it is understood today *i.e.*, to provide for all aspects of urban living.

Land Acquisition and Disposal

The basic legal instrument to achieve the objective of supplying land for public purpose and urban development is the Land Acquisition Act, 1894. This law enables acquisition of private land for public purpose. Since most of the land in India is in private ownership, certain fundamental legal issues are involved in the achievement of this policy objective, namely :

(i) restriction of private rights over land;
(ii) acquisition of private land has to be for a public purpose;
(iii) land can be acquired only through the agency of the State Government; and
(iv) compensation must be paid to the person/persons whose land is acquired.

The instrument of large-scale acquisition of private land has been justified on the following assumptions:

(i) underdeveloped land at the periphery of a growing city acquired by a public authority at relatively low prices (prevailing agricultural prices) would have the effect of preventing undesirable speculation likely to occur if agricultural lands are converted for urban uses.
(ii) all increases in land values would accrue to the benefit of the public.
(iii) land can be made available to the poor who can not compete in the private market at affordable prices.
(iv) land will become available to the pubic sector for purposes of development and this would also help in the orderly planning and development of the city.

The following comments can be made on the operation of the instrument of Land Acquisition.

(a) Over the years, a considerable quantity of land has been made available for the purpose of urban development all over the country—for housing, roads, railways, industrial estates and other public uses. The case of Delhi is often cited where the "Scheme for Large Scale Acquisition, Development and Disposal of Land", initiated in 1961 resulted in acquisition and utilisation of substantial tracts of land. The Delhi example has also been increasingly used as a model for urban development measures in other growing cities (Howland, 1975; Jha, 1983; Mishra, 1986).

(b) There have, however, been serious problems in operating the Land Acquisition Law. Enormous delay is caused in following all the procedures prescribed. The issue of notifications, their publication in gazette, enquiries to be conducted etc., are time consuming. Further, land owners reluctant to part with their land approach courts on some legal issue or the other and stall acquisition proceedings. At times, the action of Land Acquisition Authorities is also fraught with legal infirmities.

(c) A major bone of contention between the State and the private land owner has been the payment of compensation. A complex legal issue, it has attracted a number of court decisions. In the Bella Banerjee case, the Supreme Court held that the word 'compensation' according to Article 31(2) meant 'just equivalent' or 'what the owner has been deprived of' and insisted on full indemnification of the expropriated owner. This led to the Constitution IV Amendment Act, 1955 by which the adequacy of compensation was made non-justiciable. In the Bank Nationalisation case, the Supreme Court held that the 'object of the principle of evaluation must be to pay to the owner what he has lost', including the benefit of advantages, present as well as future. By the 25th Amendment to the Constitution, the term 'compensation' in Article 31 was substituted by the term 'amount'. Consequent on this amendment, the property of a citizen can be acquired for a public purpose by paying an amount which is less than 'just equivalent' in money or less than the market value of the property to be acquired. However, subsequent court rulings have not enabled the acquisition of property for less than the market value.

(d) An important consequence of public acquisition of land has been that the public authority is able to offer the land at very low prices. "The resulting intensity of land use, born of the fact that land has been bought cheap, is highly wasteful, uneconomic and inefficient." (Planning Commission, 1983) It has been argued that the inefficient allocation of publicly acquired land gives rise to a number of problems. For instance, there is no rational way of determining the prices at different locations. The density and development norms prescribed by public authorities tend to be lavish and result in higher transport and service costs. "Even when acquisition is possible, control is not certain, nor is there automatic assurance that the ultimate development is efficient or equitable" (Rivkin, 1983).

(e) After land is acquired, it is developed and disposed of by public authorities according to certain rules or guidelines. The method of disposal of land is generally the leasehold system according to which land is leased for a specified period of time to an individual or organisation. The lease period may extend from ten years (Bangalore) to 99 years (Delhi). The policy of long-term lease practised in Delhi is expected to achieve a greater degree of control over the use of land, collection of ground rent on a continuous basis and capture of a portion of land value increment to public account at the time of transfer. This system has, however, been criticised as restricting the spatial mobility of people and encouraging illegal transactions.

(f) Another aspect of land disposal relates to the allocation of public land to different categories of people and for different purposes. Bulk of the land allocated for residential use is usually apportioned among the low, middle and high income groups at fixed prices. Land for commercial purposes is sold in public auction with a view to obtain the best price. There is, however, a general criticism that the land distribution policy has benefited the better off sections of society more than the weaker sections.

Urban Land Ceiling

The policy of Government to bring about equitable distribution of land in urban areas was given shape in the form of legislation in 1976 when the Urban Land (Ceiling and Regulation) Act was passed. In order to achieve this objective as also to "prevent concentration of urban land in the hands of a few persons and speculation and profiteering", the law imposes certain restrictions on the holding and transfer of land.

Ceiling Limit

The Act prescribes the ceiling limit to hold vacant land by a person as follows:

(a) where the vacant land is situated in an urban agglomeration (UA) falling within category 'A', specified in Schedule-I to the Act - 500 sq. mtrs.
(b) Where the land is situated in category 'B' UA[4]—1,000 sq. mtrs.
(c) Where the land is situated in category 'C' UA—1,500 sq. mtrs.
(d) Where the land is situated in category 'D' UA—2,000 sq. mtrs.[5]

A ceiling has also been imposed on the size of the building to be constructed by any person. In an urban agglomeration within category 'A' or 'B', a building with dwelling unit cannot exceed a plinth area of 300 sq. mtrs. and in category 'C' or 'D' agglomeration, the limit is 500 sq. mtrs.

Restriction on Transfer

The Act places certain restrictions on the transfer and use of urban properties. According to Section 26, notice has to be given to the Competent Authority before transfer of vacant land within the ceiling limit by way of sale, mortgage, gift, lease or in any other manner and the Competent Authority shall have the first option to purchase the land on behalf of the State Government as per the price calculated under the provisions of the Land Acquisition Act. If such option is not exercised within a period of sixty days, the person concerned will be at liberty to dispose of the land to whomsoever he may like. Section 27 of the Act provides for obtaining previous permission of the Competent Authority in respect of transfers of any urban or urbanisable land with a building. However, this provision (Section 27) is not in operation at present in view of certain Court rulings.

The operation of the Urban Land Ceiling Law has been very much at variance with the stated objectives. The Act has failed to prevent concentration of ownership of urban land to achieve equitable distribution. A critical evaluation of its implementation would reveal the following:

(a) The Act suffers from certain anomalies like vague definitions giving scope for ambiguous interpretations, and provisions difficult to enforce.
(b) Determination of surplus land is not easy in case of lands with buildings or where the ownership vests in more than one person.

(c) The compensation to be paid for the land acquired under the ULC Act is very meagre—a maximum of Rs. 10 as against the market value under the Land Acquisition Act.

(d) The discretionary power vested in the State Government to grant exemption to any person on grounds of hardship (Section 20) has resulted in a large number of applications for exemption. This has contributed to delay in determination of surplus land as a decision on exemption has to precede the decision on acquiring surplus land. There is also the criticism that the power to grant exemption has been exercised arbitrarily.

(e) Proper implementation of the Act could have perhaps resulted in substantial surplus land becoming available in large cities for planned development and cheeking speculative land dealing. Unfortunately, the consequences have been more negative. Initially, the new law had an adverse effect on construction activity but subsequently it started breeding corruption as professional land dealers began exploiting the legal loopholes on the one hand and the discretionary power vested in government on the other.

The Urban Land Ceiling Act is a classic case of a well conceived legislation with all the elements of progressive policy failing to achieve its objectives. "Because of the manner in which it has been drafted and implemented, the Act has not achieved any of the objectives for which it was enacted.' (National Commission on Urbanisation, 1987). Successful implementation of the Act could have also helped reorganisation of land use patterns in the cities. A good opportunity to achieve the goals of Urban Land Policy—optimum social use of land, equitable distribution and augmented supply of land in the market seems to have been lost.

Taxation

In India, taxation has hardly been used as an instrument of land policy. Taxes on land and property have been conceived primarily as sources of revenue to the local bodies. The income so derived is no doubt important to provide the basic municipal services in cities.

The major tax levied by all municipal authorities in India is the property tax which is based on the annual rental value of land and buildings[6] Its effectiveness even as an instrument of revenue generation, however, seems to be declining. The share of property and related taxes in municipal revenue was 40 to 56 per cent in 1976-77 (Dutta, 1984) but declined to 23 per cent in 1979-80 (World Bank, 1986). The operation of this tax suffers from several constraints, the chief of which is its linkage to rent control legislation.

Tax on vacant land is levied in some cities like Calcutta and Madras. However, this instrument has not proved effective either in inducing more efficient land use or in checking speculation owing to low rates and weak administration (Acharya, 1988). Betterment levies and development charges are imposed by some municipal and development authorities but they have had only limited success in India, primarily owing to low levy rates and to low valuation of properties (World Bank, 1986).

It is possible to employ taxation as an effective instrument of Urban Land Policy in India—to increase the supply of land needed for urban development, to promote efficient utilisation of land and to recover some of the land value increases resulting from public investment.

IMPACT OF POLICY NATURES

The overall impact of Urban Land Policy measures in India (with degrees of variation between cities) has been more negative than positive. None of the objectives specified earlier has been fulfilled. The only objective where success to a limited extent has been achieved is in the supply of developed land for the purpose of housing and certain other development schemes. Even here, the demand is outpatient the supply, although there has been considerable public investment in land acquisition and development.

A major failure has been in the area of controlling the rising land prices. Majority of the urban dwellers, especially the poor cannot afford to buy land in the open market. The public authorities are unable to supply adequate land at reasonable prices. The available public land is not put to efficient use. Land use controls seem to have exercised more of a negative influence on efficient land management. Unauthorised developments and large scale infringement of building regulations are reflective of unimaginative rules on the one hand and poor enforcement on the other.

A serious criticism of the Urban Land Policy measures is that they have favoured the rich at the cost of the poor. This is illustrated by separation of land uses, dispersal of employment opportunities and the acquisition of urban fringe land for public purposes. Questions have been asked as to how far the acquisition of land in the urban fringe (purchased at low agricultural use prices) for high income housing, commercial development or for the beautification of the city can be justified in terms of public purposes (Planning Commission, 1983).

The failure of many of the measures undertaken so far brings out the complexity of the land problems on the one hand and the inability of the authorities to adequately deal with them on the other. This poses a serious challenge to the policy makers in India.

NOTES

1. The Urban Land (Ceiling & Regulation) Act, 1976.
2. Entry No. 17 in List II of Seventh Schedule.
3. Entry No. 42 in List III of Seventh Schedule.
4. UA—Urban Agglemoration.
5. Urban Agglomeration have been classified as A, B, C & D in Schedule I to the ULC Act. The four largest cities of Bombay, Calcutta, Delhi and Madras have been Classified as 'A'. The other large cities like Ahmedabad, Bangalore, Hyderabad, Kanpur and Pune are classified as 'B'. Similar cities have further been categorised as 'C' and 'D'.
6 Details of Land Tax System have been discussed in Chapter 8.

4

BANGALORE : THE STUDY AREA

Bangalore, the capital city of Karnataka, was founded by Kempe Gowda I in 1537. It lies in the heart of the Deccan Peninsula at an elevation of 900 metres. Located at 12.58 North latitude and 77.33 East longitude, the city is physically situated on a ridge top running from west to east. This ridge divides the region into two distinct river valleys, *viz.*, the South Pennar region sloping towards the east and the Arkavathy basin sloping towards the south-west. The city is almost equidistant from sea coast on either side—the eastern and the western. It lies at a distance of 357 km. from Madras on the east and 390 km. from Mangalore on the west (**Fig. 4.1**). It occupies a central position in the Southern India.

THE SURROUNDING REGION

Bangalore city forms part of Bangalore district (**Fig. 4.2**) which is situated in the southeastern corner of Karnataka State. Though the smallest district of Karnataka in area (2,191 sq. km.), it has the largest population (3.5 million). The urban population constitutes 84 per cent of the total population of the district while the remaining 16 per cent inhabit 718 villages. Bangalore is surrounded by Bangalore Rural District[1] on all sides except a small part on the south and east which is bounded by Dharmapuri District of Tamil Nadu.

Administratively, Bangalore district is divided into three taluks—Bangalore North, Bangalore South and Anekal. While Bangalore North and South taluks are headquartered in Bangalore city, the headquarters of Anekal taluk is located at Anekal town, situated almost in the southeastern corner of the district. Yelahanka to the north and Kengeri to the South-East were planned to be developed as satellite towns. The former has almost become a part of Bangalore city while the latter, where Bangalore University is located, is in the process of becoming so. Bommasandra, Jigani, Attibele and Anekal towards the south-east and Peenya towards the west house industrial estates, the last named being one of the biggest in India.

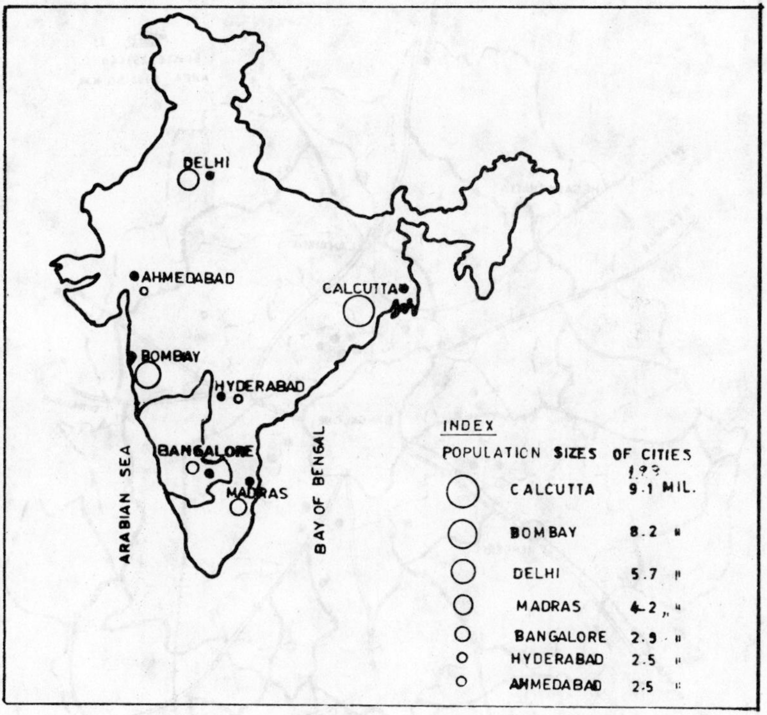

Fig 4.1 : Position of Bangalore City in India

Source : Census of India 1981

While the area comprising Bangalore district beyond the city may be said to constitute the city's immediate hinterland, viewed in the larger regional context, the area within a radius of 70 km. can be considered the 'zone of influence' of metropolitan Bangalore. It may be seen from **Fig. 4.3** that a number of urban centres do this region—the important ones being Doddaballapur and Chickballapur to the North, Hosakote and Malur to the east, Kunigal to the west, Ramanagaram and Channapatna to the south-west and Kanakapura to the South. Some of them like Channapatna and Kanakapura are fast growing towns. The urban growth of this region has an important bearing on the spatial planning of Bangalore from a regional perspective.

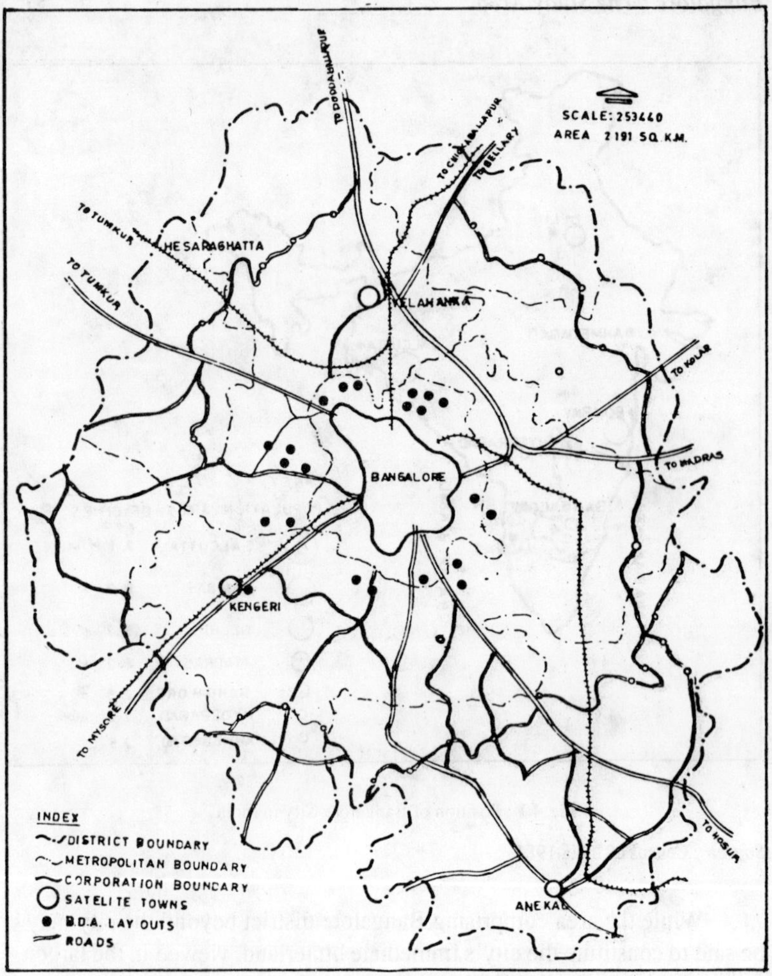

Fig 4.2 : Map of Bangalore District

Source : Department of Town Planning Karnataka

Natural Resources

In the absence of any major river, tanks and wells constitute the main water resources of the region. There are about 461 tanks with a surface water potential of 12,541 hectares accounting for 54 per cent of the total water resources of Bangalore district. Ground water can be tapped at a

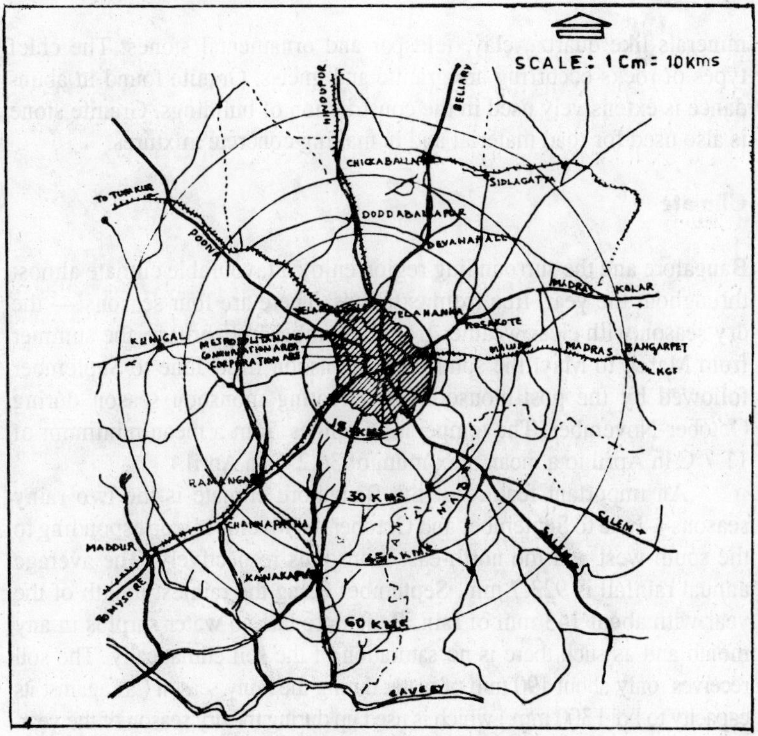

Fig. 4.3 : Bangalore : Regional Setting

Source : **Based on Ramegowda K.S. (1986) : Urban and Regional Planning**

depth of one to three metres in low lying areas and ten metres in certain areas. Open wells numbering 7,741 mostly go dry in summer. There are also 3,921 borewells. The total groundwater potential of the district is about 11,220 hectares.

The forest resources in the region are meagre with the forest area (4,203) forming just 1.92 per cent of the total area of the district. The climatic and topographical features of the region favour the growth of a variety of plants. Though no major forest produce is available, there are species which yield timber like tamarind, jack fruit, honge and eucalyptus. Trees which are useful for use as firewood are found extensively. The Bannerghatta National Park situated at a distance of 22 km. from Bangalore was established to develop and preserve the existing flora and fauna of the region.

The region is poor in mineral resources. There are hardly any mineral deposits of commercial importance in the area, except small deposits of minor minerals like quartz., clay, feldspar and ornamental stones. The chief types of rocks occurring are granite and gneiss. Granite found in abundance is extensively used in the construction of buildings. Granite stone is also used for road material and in making concrete mixtures.

Climate

Bangalore and the surrounding region enjoy a favourable climate almost throughout the year, free from extremes. There are four seasons — the dry season with clear weather from December to February, the summer from March to May, the south-west monsoon from June to September followed by the post-monsoon or retreating monsoon season during October-November. The temperature ranges from a mean minimum of 11.7°C in April to a mean maximum of 36.2°C in April.

An important feature of the Bangalore climate is the two rainy seasons—June to September and October to November, corresponding to the south-west and the north-east monsoons respectively. The average annual rainfall is 923.7 mm, September being the rainiest month of the year with about 143 mm of rain. Bangalore has no water surplus in any month and as such there is no saturation of the soil climatically. The soil receives only about 190 mm of water during the rainy season (as against its capacity to hold 300 mm) which is used up during the dry season of the year. This accounts for the water deficiency experienced by Bangalore.

Urbanisation causes changes in climatic elements. The heat balance of the region altered by the loss of fields and forests and the emergence of asphalt roads and concrete buildings and local heat production from combustion, all resulting in what is known as the 'urban heat island'. A mobile survey of air temperature and humidity over the Bangalore urban area carried out in April and May 1977 revealed that the temperatures in built up areas were in excess of those in suburbs by about 2°C. The survey repeated in December and in January 1986 showed a higher temperature in crowded areas than those in Cubbon Park and Lalbagh by 2.5°C in the mornings and 3.2°C in the afternoon.

Agricultural Economy

Agriculture constitutes the main occupation of the people in the rural hinterland. The major crops cultivated are paddy, ragi and pulses. As there are no major rivers, the irrigation potential in the district is quite low. The area irrigated by tanks and wells is about 18.5 per cent of the net area sown. The soils in the area vary from red laterite and red fine loamy to clayey type. Vegetables and fruits are grown on a large scale and horticulture contributes substantially to the economy of the district.

The land utilisation pattern of Bangalore district reveals that the net area under cultivation in 1987-88 was 47.07 per cent and the area under non-agricultural use constituted 21.7 per cent. Fallow lands accounted for 15.48 per cent and barren and uncultivable land 4.02 per cent. Permanent pastures formed 4.7 per cent of the total area and the balance came under miscellaneous uses.

Land holdings are small, with as much as 73.6 per cent of the holdings being less than 5 acres. Large holdings with an extent of 50 acres and more form just 0.2 per cent of the total holdings. The average size of a holding declined from 4.65 acres in 1971 to 4.37 acres in 1976 which is evidence of the process of fragmentation of agricultural holdings and conversion to non-agricultural category under the influence of urbanisation.

On the whole, it may be observed that Bangalore has a poor rural hinterland and a surrounding region with a physical topography that allows for expansion on all sides.

URBAN EXPANSION

Bangalore city has expanded considerably since the days of Kempe Gowda who set outer limits to the growth of the city by erecting four watch towers at cardinal points in different directions—Hebbal tank in the North, Lalbagh hillock in the South, Ulsoor tank in the East and Kempambudhi tank in the West. The city has grown far beyond these 'Kempe Gowda towers' as can be seen in **Fig. 4.4**. The same figure shows the urban spread of Bangalore from the time of its founding in 1537 when the city used to be called 'pete' (market in Kannada). In fact, Bangalore happened to be a major manufacturing and trading centre at that time.

With the coming of the British in the 19th century, the city began to expand rapidly. A Civil and Military Station was founded in the eastern part of the city. The development of this part of the city was oriented towards providing for the military needs of the British, as also housing and institutional facilities. Residential localities like Frazer town, Richmond town and Tasker Town were developed in what came to be called the Cantonment area. New residential extensions were also developed in the older part of the city area—like Malleswaram, Visveswarapuram, Basavanagudi. While the Cantonment area came under the direct control of the British, the city portion continued to be under the jurisdiction of the Maharaja of Mysore.

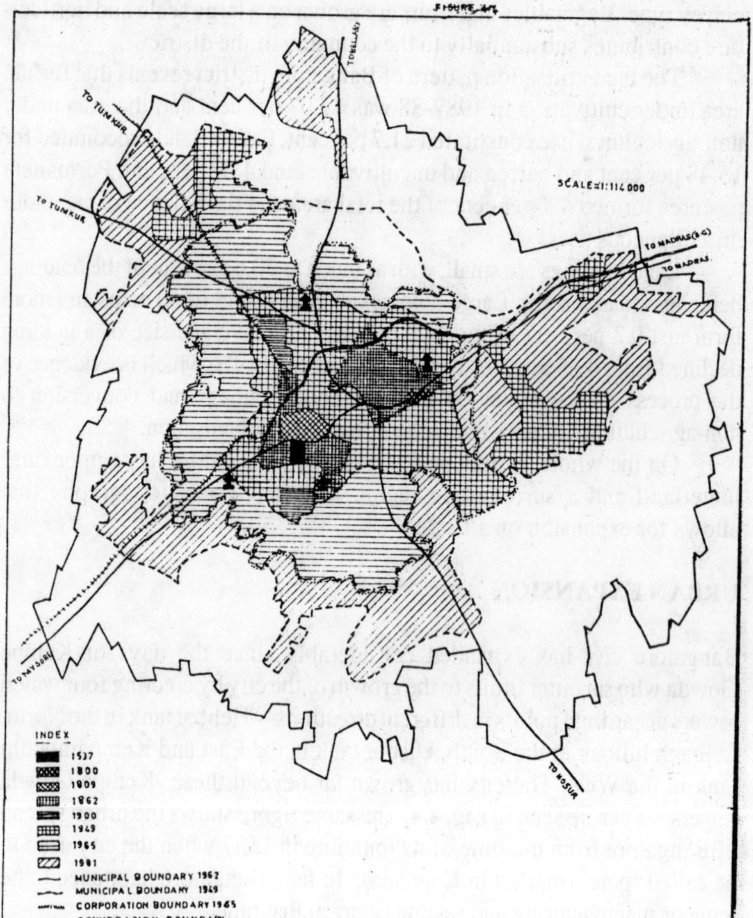

Fig. 4.4 : Bangalore : Urban Spread

The last decade of the 19th century and the first two decades of the 20th century witnessed a rapid growth of new extensions. The city began spreading simultaneously northward and southward. In 1892, two extensions were added—Seshadripuram (north-west from Race Course Road) and Chamarajpet (South westward from Fort). In 1898, Basavanagudi to the south and Malleswaram to the north-east were formed. Frazer Town was established in 1912, Sriramapuram and Gavipuram in 1915 and Visveswarapuram in 1918. During the years 1922-23, the number of extensions further increased—Guttahalli, Tasker Town, Cox Town and Austin Town. Venkatarangapura was added in 1925 and Gandhinagar in 1930. Kumara Park and Narasimharaja Colony were formed in 1938. With the formation of the Bangalore City Improvement Trust in 1945, expansion of the city came to be planned on a large scale. New extensions came into existence - Kumara Park West and Wilson Garden in 1947, Vyalikaval and Sunkenahalli in 1948 and Jayamahal in 1949.

The two urban settlements — City and Cantonment — which developed as independent entities finally merged into a single urban centre in 1949 when the Bangalore City Municipal Corporation came into being. In 1956 Bangalore became the capital of the reorganised larger State of Mysore. The Bangalore Development Authority which was set up in 1976 began planning and forming new layouts in different directions of the city resulting in further expansion.

The area of Bangalore City proper increased from 28.85 sq. kms. in 1901 to 151 sq. kms. in 1981—a five fold rise. The Urban Agglomeration of 1981 (which included 17 towns and 79 outgrowths) covered a much bigger area of 365.65 sq. km. The Plan for the Metropolitan Area drawn up in 1984 covered an extent of 1,279 sq. km. which included a conurbation area of nearly 440 sq. km.

It needs to be pointed out here that there is some confusion about the precise area and population while referring to Bangalore city as such. The concepts used to denote the different jurisdictional areas, administrative and territorial, in and around Bangalore are as follows :

> 'Corporation area' is the area coming under the jurisdiction of the Bangalore City Municipal Corporation.
>
> The concept of 'Urban Agglomeration' adopted in the Census of 1971 and 1981 represents 'a contiguous urban spread constituting a town and its adjoining urban outgrowths or two or more physically contiguous towns together with contiguous well reorganised urban outgrowths, which may actually fall within the revenue limits of a village or villages' (Census of India, 1981).

The 'BDA area' (City Improvement Trust Board area prior to 1976) includes the extensions and layouts under the jurisdiction of the Bangalore Development Authority (**Fig. 4.2**).

The 'Metropolitan Area' or 'Planning Area' concept adopted by the planners refers to the Local Planning Area declared as such under the Karnataka Town and Country Planning Act. The area that is built up and is earmarked as urbanisable is called the 'conurbation area'.

The spatial growth of the city may be attributed to three major factors : (a) increase in population due to immigration or natural growth, (b) absence of natural boundaries to the physical expansion of the city, and (c) changes in the administrative boundaries of the city.

DEMOGRAPHIC FEATURES

Growth in Population

In 1901, the population of Bangalore was 0.23 million. By 1981, it had risen to 2.9 million—an increase of 2.7 million or 13 times in 80 years (**Table 4.1**). During the same period, the share of Bangalore in the total urban population of the State, increased from less than 14 per cent to 27 per cent. The State of Karnataka itself witnessed a rising trend in urbanisation during this period. The urban population of the State increased from 13 per cent to about 29 per cent and the number of Class I cities which was confined to just one (Bangalore) in the first decade of the century rose to 17 by 1981. But the primacy of Bangalore in the State in quite high—being five times larger than the second ranking city of Hubli-Dharwad. On the national scene, Bangalore achieved the status of a million-plus city in 1961 and ranked seventh among the nine million-plus cities during the period 1951-71. By 1981, it came to occupy the fifth position overtaking Hyderabad and Ahmedabad.

An analysis of the decade-wise growth in the population of Bangalore (**Table 4.1**) reveals that the decade 1971-81 recorded a high growth rate of 76 per cent, which was the highest for any metropolitan city in India during that decade. However, the momentum for the growth of the city actually started in the 1940s. The highest growth rate of the city (94%) was witnessed during the decade 1941-51. The unusually high growth rate during that period was mainly on account of industrialisation and the wartime scarcity conditions in rural areas leading to migration. During

TABLE 4.1 : **Decade-wise variation in population of Bangalore**

Year	*Metroplitan Area (in million)*	*%age increase*	*City Corporation (in million)*	*%age increase*	*Mmetroplitan Area Excluding Corporation*		*Per cent metroplitan area population to total urban population of State*
					Popul-tion	*%age increase*	
1901	0.23	—	0.16	—	0.07	—	13.90
1911	0.26	14.50	0.19	19.20	0.06	1.50	16.60
1921	0.31	19.20	0.24	25.40	0.07	4.20	16.90
1931	0.40	27.50	0.31	29.10	0.09	23.90	17.70
1941	0.51	28.90	0.41	32.60	0.10	17.00	18.50
1951	0.99	94.90	0.78	91.60	0.21	108.70	22.30
1961	1.21	21.40	0.91	16.70	0.30	40.80	22.90
1971	1.66	37.00	1.42	56.90	0.23	22.20	23.40
1981	2.91	76.70	2.48	74.60	0.43	86.00	27.20

Source : Comprehensive Development Plan, Report of Bangalore, 1984.

the first-four decades of this century, the Corporation area registered a higher rate of population growth compared to the periphery (Metropolitan area excluding the Corporation area). From 1941 onwards, however, the periphery began to witness faster growth.

Between 1951 and 1961, the population increase in the periphery was over 40 per cent as against 16 per cent in the Corporation area. In contrast, during the next decade 1961-71, the population in the Corporation area increased by nearly 57 per cent, whereas, the growth in the periphery was only about 22 per cent. This can be explained by the addition of new areas to the Corporation limits during the sixties. Between 1971 and 1981, the periphery again registered a higher growth rate of 86 per cent compared to 74 per cent in the Corporation area. During the period of 30 years from 1951 to 1981, the outer edge of peripheral area registered a higher growth rate compared to the City Corporation area and the metropolitan area as a whole, except for the period 1961-71. It is also observed that during this period of 30 years, the population of metropolitan area as well as the peripheral area more than trebled itself.

Migration

One of the important factors contributing to the growth in the population of Bangalore is inmigration. In 1971, the number of life-time migrants in Bangalore Urban Agglomeration was estimated at 610,795 constituting about

36.7 per cent of the total population. In 1981, the number of migrants increased to 1,099,086 accounting for 37.7 per cent of the population.

Although migrants come to Bangalore from all parts of India, the vast majority of them come from the four southern states (**Table 4.2**). The largest number of people migrate from within the State of Karnataka itself. The percentage of such migrants was 56.6 per cent in 1971 and moved up to 59.4 per cent in 1981. Here again, those migrants from within the district of Bangalore went up from about 18 per cent to 20 per cent and those

TABLE 4.2 : **Percentage distribution of life time migrants to Bangalore Urban Agglomeration**

(percentage)

Local Residence	*1971*			*1981*		
	Persons	*Male*	*Female*	*Persons*	*Male*	*Female*
Elsewhere in District of enumeration						
Total	18.60	19.00	18.20	20.60	19.70	21.60
Rural	29.70	27.30	32.80	32.80	30.90	35.10
Urban	11.00	13.50	7.90	9.60	9.20	9.90
In other Districts of State						
Total	38.00	36.90	39.40	38.80	39.00	38.60
Rural	35.70	35.90	35.50	34.80	35.90	33.60
Urban	40.30	38.20	43.00	43.00	42.50	43.60
Beyond State of enumeration : Andhra Pradesh						
Total	6.90	6.60	7.20	7.00	6.80	7.20
Rural	7.30	7.20	7.50	6.60	6.40	6.90
Urban	6.70	6.40	7.20	7.50	7.40	7.60
Kerala						
Total	6.00	6.90	4.90	6.10	6.80	5.30
Rural	5.20	6.20	3.90	6.30	7.00	5.40
Urban	6.70	7.50	5.80	6.00	6.80	5.30
Tamil Nadu						
Total	21.30	20.20	22.70	20.80	20.60	20.90
Rural	17.80	17.60	18.00	16.40	16.40	16.30
Urban	24.20	22.20	26.50	25.10	24.90	25.10
Other States						
Total	8.20	9.50	6.50	6.00	6.40	5.80
Rural	4.30	5.80	2.30	3.10	3.40	2.70
Urban	11.10	12.20	9.60	8.80	9.20	8.50
Outside India	1.00	0.90	1.10	0.70	0.70	0.60
Total	10.00	100.00	100.00	100.00	100.00	100.00
Rural	41.70	41.00	41.660	42.60	48.90	45.90
Urban	58.30	58.10	57.30	57.80	50.40	53.40

Source : Census of India, 1971 and 1981.

coming from the other districts of Karnataka constituted about 38 per cent. The other three southern states of Andhra Pradesh, Kerala and Tamil Nadu together account for about 33 per cent of the migrants. The highest contribution out of these three states is from Tamil Nadu, *i.e.*, about 21 per cent, while Andhra Pradesh and Kerala contribute about 6 to 7 per cent each. The rest of the states in India accounted for 8 per cent of the migrants in 1971 and this figure declined to 6 per cent in 1981. People outside India contributed a small percentage of 1 in 1971, which further declined to 0.7 per cent in 1981.

It is significant to note that more people have migrated from urban areas (58%) than from rural areas (42%). From the district of Bangalore itself, understandably, there is much greater inflow from the rural areas. This trend also indicates that people living in smaller towns want to move to bigger towns.

The number of males migrating to Bangalore is more than the number of females—the former accounting for 55.5 per cent and the latter 44.5 per cent in 1971. In 1981, however, the gap narrowed down, the corresponding percentages being 53 and 47. It is also observed that in 1981, a larger number of females has moved in from within Bangalore district, particularly from rural areas. Similarly, from Andhra Pradesh and Tamil Nadu, the percentage of female migrants is slightly higher than that of male migrants.

An analysis of the reasons for migration to Bangalore reveals that the largest number migrates for the purpose of employment (30 %), followed by the family being moved (29%), marriage (18%) and education (6%). About 17 per cent of the people have migrated for various other reasons (**Table 4.3**). The pattern of distribution of migrants is more or less similar from all the states, except that the reason of family being moved constitutes a higher percentage amongst the migrants from within Bangalore district and other states of India, excluding the three southern states. From the state of Kerala, employment constitutes the most important pull factor accounting for as much as over 43 per cent of its migrants. While employment constitutes the most important reason for migration amongst males (50%), marriage accounts for the highest number of female migrants (37%).

Density of Population

A good indicator of the city's demographic pressure is the density of population. The gross density of Bangalore city which was as low as 13 per acre in 1911 rose to 46 per acre in 1951 and had hovered around

TABLE 4.3 : **Reasons for Migration to Bangalore Urban Agglomeration, 1981**

	Employment			*Education*			*Family moved*			*Marriage*			*Others*		
Last residence	*person*	*male*	*female*	*persons*	*male*	*female*	*persons*	*male*	*female*	*persons*	*male*	*female*	*persons*	*male*	*female*
Total	24.80	44.10	4.70	6.40	9.30	3.30	26.20	22.00	30.40	20.50	1.10	40.60	22.20	23.40	20.90
Rural	25.30	44.80	4.70	6.10	9.20	2.80	25.90	21.70	30.30	20.60	1.10	41.80	22.10	23.10	21.00
Urban	23.20	42.00	4.60	7.10	9.50	4.80	27.00	23.00	30.90	20.20	1.20	38.90	22.40	24.20	20.70
In other districts of state															
Total	29.70	50.50	6.20	7.20	9.80	4.30	29.00	22.80	35.90	18.00	0.50	37.70	16.10	16.40	15.80
Rural	33.20	54.70	5.70	8.00	11.20	4.00	25.30	18.60	33.90	18.50	0.50	41.50	14.90	15.00	14.80
Urban	27.20	47.10	6.50	6.60	8.60	4.50	31.60	26.20	37.30	17.60	0.50	35.20	17.00	17.50	16.50
Beyond State of enumeration															
Andhra Pradesh															
Total	29.40	51.50	6.00	6.20	86.70	3.50	30.30	23.00	38.00	19.30	1.00	38.90	14.70	15.70	13.60
Rural	31.70	55.10	5.90	5.20	7.70	2.50	29.00	21.60	37.20	20.50	1.00	42.10	13.50	14.60	12.20
Urban	27.60	48.50	6.00	6.90	9.50	4.30	31.40	24.30	38.60	18.40	0.90	36.30	15.70	16.70	14.90
Kerala															
Total	43.40	65.20	11.70	7.70	7.60	7.90	21.70	13.20	34.10	13.40	0.50	32.00	13.80	13.50	14.20
Rural	45.60	67.40	11.70	8.70	8.40	9.10	19.40	11.20	32.00	13.20	0.40	33.00	13.20	12.60	14.20
Urban	41.20	63.00	11.60	6.80	6.90	6.90	24.00	15.10	36.00	13.50	0.50	31.10	14.40	14.50	14.20
Tamil Nadu															
Total	32.30	55.30	6.90	3.70	4.50	2.80	29.50	22.60	37.30	18.90	0.90	38.90	15.450	16.70	14.10
Rural	35.70	58.40	8.20	3.40	3.90	2.80	28.30	21.30	36.70	18.10	0.90	39.00	14.50	15.60	13.30
Urban	30.30	53.20	6.10	3.90	5.00	2.80	30.30	23.40	37.60	19.40	0.90	38.90	16.00	17.60	14.60
Other States															
Total	26.20	42.90	6.30	6.20	9.40	4.40	38.10	27.60	50.90	11.40	0.60	24.20	17.10	19.50	14.10
Rural	31.60	49.30	6.30	83.0	9.30	9.30	11.40	20.80	39.60	14.10	0.50	33.70	17.50	20.10	13.60
Urban	25.20	41.70	6.40	7.30	9.50	4.30	40.50	39.30	53.50	10.60	0.60	21.80	16.50	18.70	13.90
Outside India	20.10	30.70	6.20	11.90	17.10	5.00	31.20	22.30	45.00	8.20	0.70	18.00	27.60	29.10	25.20
Total															
Total	29.80	50.70	6.30	6.30	8.40	3/90	28.70	22.20	36.00	18.00	0.80	37.50	17.10	17.90	16.30
Rural	31.60	52.90	6.10	6.50	8.90	3.60	26.00	19.80	33.40	18.80	0.80	40.40	17.20	17.70	15.50

Source : Census of India, 1981

that figure till 1981. For the Corporation area, however, the density had reached 65 per acre. The ODP was drawn for a density of 35 persons per acre in 1981 and 48 persons per acre in 2001 in the metropolitan area. While the city maintained its overall low gross density level over the decades, the intra-city variations in density have been sharp, varying from less than 30 per acre to over 300 per acre in 1981.

Fig. 4.5 shows the intra-city variations in density. The spatial pattern of population distribution in Bangalore has over the years revealed bi-nodality. There are two population foci—one near the City Market [Cubbon

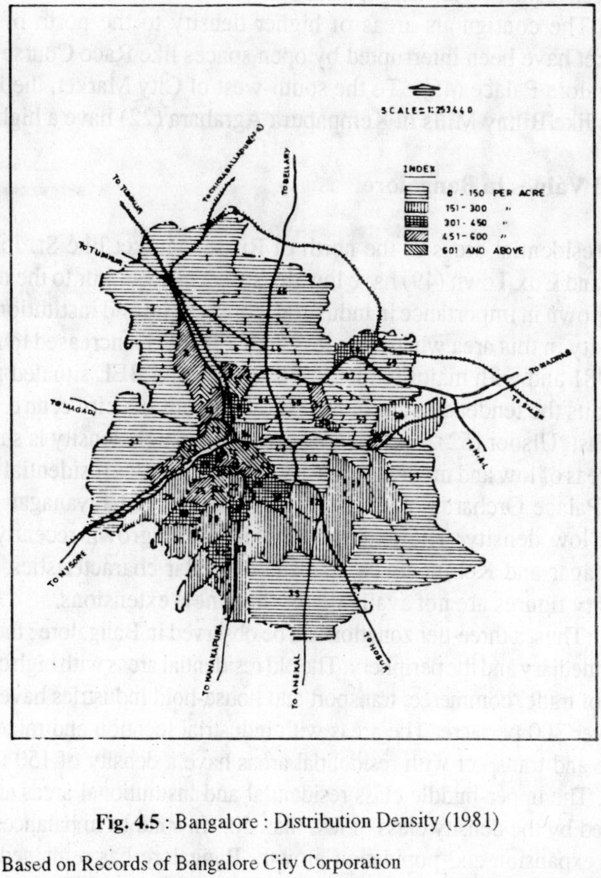

Fig. 4.5 : Bangalore : Distribution Density (1981)

Source : Based on Records of Bangalore City Corporation

pet $(42)^2$ density 386 per acre] and the other near Russel Market [Central Bazar (57): density 338 per acre]. These two foci are separated by low density area (about 50 per acre) like Vidhana Soudha (43) and Tasker Town (59). While the two focal areas have the highest population concentration in space (with 8 per cent of population concentrated in one per cent ofthe area in 1971), the 'crater' or the low density areas which breaks the contiguity of the most congested areas of the city, has open spaces such as Cubbon Park and Paradegrounds and institutions like High Court, Vidhana Soudha, General Post Office and All India Radio. This low density 'crater' was the result of the amalgamation of the city and cantonment areas and the growth of administrative and educational institutions with extensive open spaces in between (Prakash Rao and Tewari, 1971).

The contiguous areas of higher density to the north of the City Market have been interrupted by open spaces like Race Course (44) and Bangalore Palace (45). To the south-west of City Market, the industrial areas like Binny Mills in Kempapura Agrahara (22) have a high density.

Land Values in Bangalore

The residential areas to the north of Russel Market like St. John's Hill (47) and Cox Town (49) have low density. Yeshwantpur to the north-east has grown in importance in industrial, commercial and institutional fields. Density in this area which was less than 7 in 1971, increased to nearly 39 in 1981 and with major industries like HMT and BEL situated nearby, it exhibits the tendency of assuming the functions o a city centre. Towards the east, Ulsoor (52), a residential area with a high density is surrounded by areas of low and moderate density. The prestigious residential localities like Palace Orchards (45), High Grounds (44) and Jayanagar (35)—all have low density. The extensions which have grown recently like Indiranagar and Koramangala also share similar characteristics, although density figures are not available for these new extensions.

Thus, a three-tier zonation can be observed in Bangalore : the core, the intermediary and the periphery. The old residential areas with high concentration of trade, commerce, transport and house-hold industries have a density of over 300 per acre. The areas with industrial location and mixed uses of trade and transport with residential areas have a density of 150 to 225 per acre. The upper-middle class residential and institutional areas are characterised by the density class of less than 50. 'In spite of imbalances between area expansion and population growth, Bangalore has remained as a low density city except near the city nuclei' (Prakash Rao, 1983).

Population Projections

The population projections for Bangalore city have been worked out in the two Master Plans prepared for the city—the ODP (1972) and the CDP (1984), by Tewari (1978) and by the United Nations (1987). The ODP going by the method adopted by the Registrar-General of Census projected the population of Bangalore Metropolitan Region for the year 1976 as 1.9 million and for 1981 as 2.16 million. As per the projections made by Tewari, the population of Bangalore city was estimated to reach 2.5 million in 1986 and that of the agglomeration 2.74 million in the same year. However, these estimates turned out to be low and the growth rate during 1971-81 (76 %) turned out to be very high. This obviously upset the earlier projections and there has been rethinking on the policy regarding the future development of Bangalore. The CDP finalised by Bangalore Development Authority in 1984 worked out the projected population using the method of arithmetical progression and according to this estimate, the population of Bangalore in the design years 1991 and 2001 would be 4.5 million and 7 million respectively. According to the projection made by the United Nations, the Bangalore Urban Agglomeration is expected to grow from 2.97 million in 1980 to 7.96 million by 2001.

The CDP has proposed to decongest the central area and encourage development in areas outside the central places excluding intensively developed areas and slums. The density projections are based on consideration of providing higher density along the suburban railway alignment to provide sufficient lead for the suburban railway. The densities proposed for 1991 range from 100 to 200 persons per acre on the western side and 100 persons on the other sides. By the year 2001, density up to 300 persons per acre is proposed in developed areas on the western and northern parts along the railway alignment and 100 persons per acre beyond the suburban railway alignment.

Occupational Structure

About 30 per cent of the total population of Bangalore in 1981 constituted the work force. Of them, 37 per cent were engaged in manufacturing, 18.5 per cent in trade and commerce, 9.5 per cent in transport, storage and communication and nearly 26 per cent in other services. Agriculture and allied activities claimed only 2.6 per cent of the population (Table 4.4).

TABLE 4.4 : **Bangalore Urban Agglolmeration — Occupational Structure : 1961, 1971 and 1981**

	Bangalore Urban Agglomeration		
	1961	*1971*	*1981*
Percentage of main worker to total population	32.44	29.50	29.76
Cultivation	5.23	0.67	0.93
Agricultural labourers	1.31	0.64	0.90
Livestock, Forestry, Plantations, Fishing, Hunting Orchards and Mining and Quarrying Allied activities	1.27	0.73	0.83
Manufacturing, processing, servicing and repairs			
— Household Industries	4.42	2.68	2.75
— Other than Household Industry	30.14	30.30	34.68
Construction	5.53	4.63	6.06
Trade and Commerce	12.60	18.38	18.56
Transport, Storage and Communications	4.94	12.23	9.49
Other Services	34.56	26.73	25.80

Source : Census of India, 1961, 1971 and 1981.

The occupational pattern in Bangalore has undergone significant changes over the years. Bangalore city and Cantonment area which constituted two distinct units before independence, exhibited different occupational patterns apart from varying languages and cultures. In 1941, those depending on non-agricultural production constituted nearly 27 per cent in cantonment and 35 per cent in the city. With the setting up of public sector industries, the difference narrowed down and agriculture which accounted for 71 per cent of the work-force of Bangalore District in 1951 contributed less than 50 per cent in 1961. Thus, there was a major shift towards industries, although trade and commerce claimed a small increase.

The shift towards trade and commerce became more visible in the sixities with an increasing proportion of workers entering this field as also areas like transport, communication and storage. The percentage of workers employed in trade and commerce went up from 12.6 per cent in 1961 to 18 per cent in 1971. Similarly, transport, storage and communication showed an increase from 5 per cent to 12 per cent during this period.

The seventies, while witnessing a period of rapid growth, showed little change in the occupational structure of the workforce in the city. The manufacturing sector (excluding household industry) showed an increase of just over one per cent from 33 per cent in 1971 to 34.6 per cent in 1981, although the same sector registered an increase of more than 3 per cent between 1961 and 1971. The workforce engaged in the household industry which came down from 4.4 per cent in 1961 to 2.7 per cent in 1971, remained more or less stationary in 1981. Construction has, however, shown an increase from 4.6 per cent in 1971 to a little over 6 per cent in 1981. During the same period, the number of those engaged in transport, storage and communication, has shown a decline from 12 to 9.5 per cent.

The occupational structure which noticed little change during the 'seventies should, however, be seen in the light of the changes in the areas comprising Bangalore Urban Agglomeration. A large number of villages were urbanised between 1971 and 1981. The proportion of workers who were cultivators or agricultural labourers in Bangalore district declined while the household industry registered only a marginal increase. This implied that a majority of the displaced agriculturists had to compete with the better educated urban workers for their livelihood.

On the whole, the occupational structure of the city reveals that its employment structure is dominated by secondary and tertiary sectors.

An analysis of areal differentiation for different occupational categories shows that workers engaged in household industries reside largely in the congested older areas of the city like Chickpet, Avenue Road and Bashyamnagar. Cubbonpet division itself has 22 per cent of these workers engaged in the household industry. These areas also have a high population density.

Industrial workers are distributed all over the city, although manufacturing activity by itself is highly segregated. A high percentage (over 35), however, reside in the western periphery in areas like Rajajinagar, Sriramapuram, Binnypet and Yeshwanthpur. Those engaged in trade, commerce, transport and communication are concentrated in the areas around city market and Russel Market. The professional and administrative classes live in places like Shankarapuram, Palace and Murphy Town (these localities were at one time peripheral, but they are today inter-mediary) and in new extensions like Jayanagar, Indiranagar and Koramangala.

EMERGING ROLE OF BANGALORE

From the position of the sixteenth largest city in India in 1941, Bangalore rose to the eighth place in 1961 and seventh in 1971, and ranked as the fifth largest city in 1981. The high growth rate of 76 per cent during 1971-81 has established its supremacy among the metropolitan centres of India.

In the regional context, Bangalore enjoys high primacy. The population of the city accounts for 7.8 per cent of the State's population and 45 per cent of the population of Bangalore district (rural and urban). More than a fifth of the urban population of Karnataka lives in Bangalore While it is five times larger than the next order city of the State, Hubli-Dharwad, it is six times larger than the next order city (Mysore) within a radius of 150 km. Bangalore district has 22 urban centres and Banglore city alone has 82 per cent of the total urban population of the district. This reveals the rural-urban dichotomy between Bangalore metropolis and its hinterland and the polarisation of activities in the city.

The rapid growth has also brought about major changes in the socio-economic structure of the city. The primary sector now accounts for only about 2.5 per cent of the workforce, whereas, the secondary sector employs 37.5 per cent and the tetriary sector 60 per cent (1971). The tertiary sector including those of the informal sectcr has become significant. The city continues to attract immigrate from its rural hinterland for various types of manual work.

Bangalore witnessed an impressive industrial growth during the last few decades. By 1983, Bangalore district had 168 large and medium sector industries employing about 1,78,000 persons. The number of small scale units registered in Bangalore in a year went up from 951 to 2,106 in 1985-86. The total number of small units registered by 1986-87 numbered 18,478 with an employment of 1,93,000 persons.

The importance of Bangalore as a financial centre is also growing. By the end of 1986, there were 510 branches of scheduled commercial banks in Bangalore which had advanced about Rs. 1,783 crore. The Bangalore centre alone accounted for 90 per cent of the advances from all the centres in the district. Institutional finance has played a major role in the industrial and commercial development of the city.

Bangalore occupies a premier place in the field of science and education. It has a number of institutions of national importance like—Indian Institute of Science, National Institute of Mental Health and Neuro Sciences, Indian Space Research Organisation, Aeronautical Development Establishment etc. The city houses a large number of engineering and medical colleges, perhaps the largest for any city in India. There are plans to set up a 'Science City' and 'Film City' in the vicinity of Bangalore. Reputed companies have set up their corporate offices here.

Of late, Bangalore has also emerged as a major convention centre in the country.

This tremendous growth has brought in its train a number of problems, particularly, in the field of infrastructure. Water, power, housing and transport have come under severe pressure. The availability of water is 435 million litres per day against the requirement of 1,080 million litres per day. The average monthly power consumption in Bangalore stood at 213 million units in 1986-87 and the demand for power has been growing rapidly. Public transport is far from adequate. This has resulted in a steep rise in the privately owned vehicles, especially two-wheelers. The average annual growth in the vehicle population during 1971-81 was 22.6 per cent as against 7.6 per cent in the population growth. The increased intensity of traffic combined with the radial pattern of roads has resulted in acute traffic congestion, particularly in and around the central business centres in the city. The provision of adequate shelter to the growing numbers, especially to the weaker sections is another serious problem confronting the planners.

Central to most of the socio-economic changes taking place in Bangalore is the problem of land—its availability as well as its efficient utilisation. The changing pattern of land use and the growing needs of the population have brought into sharp focus the need for formulating an appropriate land policy for the Bangalore Metropolitan area.

NOTES

1. Bangalore district has been subject to frequent territorial changes. In 1962, the district was divided into Bangalore Rural and Bangalors Urban. In 1966, both these districts were merged. Again in 1986 the district was bifurcated into Bangalore Rural and Bangalore (Urban) districts.
2. Figures in brackets indicate the Corporation Division No. shown in the map relating to distribution of density of population (**Fig. 4.5**). Divisions are territorial units within the Bangalore City Corporation area.

5

LAND VALUES IN BANGALORE

The issue of urban land values is complex and as noted in Chapter 2, different models have been put forward to explain the phenomenon of changing land values — that land value depends on proximity (Hurd), location (Marshall), accessibility (Haig), efficiency of uses in various locations (Ratcliff), preferences for land, goods and accessibility (Alonso) and rent paying ability of users (Northam). Each of these theories may be partially valid but none of them can fully or satisfactorily explain the behaviour of land prices in the urban land market.

FACTORS AFFECTING LAND VALUES

No single factor determines land values and the law of supply and demand does not influence the land market in the same manner as it does other commodities. Urban land can be distinguished from other goods by its unique qualities:

(a) Land is physically undepreciable and is not influenced by time, while the quality of virtually all other commodities depreciate with time.
(b) Land is not transportable. Even if the use of land can be changed, the land itself is stationary. As a land cannot be transported, the price of land is determined by the demand for land in certain areas, not by the availability and demand for land in the entire region.
(c) Land is limited in quantity and its supply cannot be increased. However, the intensity of land use can be increased. This serves as a substitute for additional quantities of land.
(d) Land is used not only for production purposes but also as a long term investment or as a mode of savings. The scarcity of land and its physically undepreciable character make it profitable to

hold large reserves without using it as a factor of production (Darin-Drabkin, 1977).

Land values are thus influenced by a variety of factors. Apart from those delineated above, there are certain other aspects like urban growth and planning and financial decisions which affect land value in a country like India. In the context of Urban Land Policy, the following factors can be identified as affecting urban land values:

Location of Land

Land location being specific, it plays a crucial part in determining the land value. The use of land for a particular activity depends on factors like accessibility, centrality, land use in adjoining areas, and availability of various amenities and services. Central locations command a higher value. Environmental factors like health and educational facilities, recreation etc., apart from other urban amenities like water supply, shopping centres, etc., contribute to determining the value of land. In the case of residential land use, socio-economic status of the population residing in the neighbourhood also affect the values significantly.

Urbanisation or rural-to-urban transition

Another significant factor contributing to the high rise of land values is the initial conversion of land at the periphery of the city from rural to urban use. Such a conversion is usually regulated through complicated procedures since it requires provision of urban services like water supply, sewerage, etc. The value of such land keeps increasing depending on the provision of infrastructural facilities in the area.

Land use Controls

The development plans and the zoning regulations control the land use in different parts of the city. The land earmarked for commercial use generally commands a higher price compared to the other uses. At times, the use of land is diverted from its stated purpose. The rigidity or flexibility with which such diversions are permitted by the authorities can affect land values. The building bye-laws and subdivision regulations are also instrumental in determining the land values. The intensity of use permitted in the land in a particular area can also cause variations in the values of land. For instance, a site where a high rise building is permitted will fetch a higher price than a site where such construction is not permitted even in the same locality.

Shortage of Serviced Land

The problem of developing countries is not merely one of availability of urban land but the availability of serviced land. Even in cities where there is scope for expansion on all sides, serviced land is in short supply in relation to demand. Acquisition and development of land and providing the necessary services is a time-consuming process. As such, serviced land in most cities fetches a high price

Financial Resources

Another constraint in developing countries is the scarcity of financial resources to provide serviced land on a scale that matches the requirements of the growing population. Land owners tend to hold land in anticipation of increase in capital values and rent. The availability of finances and the cost of such acquisition of land and buildings can therefore, affect market values.

The combined effect of the aforementioned factors result in increasing values of land in cities over time.

LAND PRICE TRENDS IN BANGALORE

Lack of reliable data is a serious handicap in any study relating to urban land values. There are no published statistics on land prices in Bangalore. Moreover, the diversified character of land prices which differ not only from one area to another area but between streets or even sites in the same area makes collection of data extremely difficult. What is attempted in this chapter is an analysis of the trends of the distribution of land values through time and space in Bangalore along with the factors influencing price formation.

For the purpose of analysing the trends in land values in the city, data were collected from the following sources :

(a) Sale statistics based on the values registered in the office of the Sub-Registrar in respect of private land transactions in selected localities;

(b) The price at which the BDA sells land to the public;
(c) Land values fixed by the State Government for different localities; and
(d) Average price estimates obtained from Real Estate agents in the city.

Trends in Land Prices based on Registered Prices

To study the changes in land prices in Bangalore city in recent years, the following eleven localities were selected in different parts of the city, each locality representing certain land use and socio-economic characteristics. The selection of localities has been done in such a way that it helps in understanding the spatial disposition of land values.

(i) Central and busy localities—Gandhinagar, Chamarajpet, Srirampuram.
(ii) Intermediate localities—Wilson Gardens, Fraser Town and Malleswaram.
(iii) City extensions—HAL II Stage, Rajajinagar, Jayanagar and Koramangala.
(iv) HIG Locality near the city centre—Sadashivanagar.

Gandhinagar is a part of the city core and is an important commercial centre. It is close to the City Railway Station, Bus Stand, Vidhana Soudha and Majestic area, which is an important commercial centre of the city.

Chamarajpet is close to the centre of the city. Although it began as a residential extension, today it has become partly commercial. It is very near to some premier institutions like Victoria and Vani Vilas Hospitals, Bangalore Medical College and is situated at a distance of about 1.5 km from the City Market area.

Wilson Gardens is situated towards the southern part and is a popular residential area for the middle class. This is at a distance of about 3 km from the city centre and is close to the National Institute of Mental Health and Neuro Sciences and MICO (Industry).

Fraser Town has developed as a residential extension in the cantonment area in the eastern part of the city. It has not developed very much over the years and houses mostly the middle class including lower middle class.

Malleswaram is located towards the western part (about 4 kms from city centre) and has developed into a major centre both in residential and commercial terms. It houses middle and upper middle classes.

HAL II Stage is a residential extension which has developed rapidly over the recent years (during 1980-89). It is very close to the Airport and has a considerable population of upper middle class, and the affluent sections.

Rajajinagar is a very large residential locality located on the western side of the city. It houses a large number of industrial workers and lower middle class people. Of late, some upper middle classes have also come to live here.

Jayanagar has developed into a major residential locality in the southern part of the city. It has a very good shopping complex and good transport facilities. It has a mixed population ranging from lower middle class to the well-to-do sections.

Koramangala is developing as a good residential extension towards the south eastern part, *i.e.*, close to Hosur Road and some industrial estates. A number of institutions like St. John's Medical College and Hospital are in this locality. Here again, the upper middle class and well-to-do sections predominate.

Sadashivanagar is regarded as a high status residential locality, fairly close to central areas like Vidhana Soudha. A large number of the affluent sections of the city population resides here.

The average land values in these localities have been calculated using the values of all sale transactions registered in the office of the Sub-Registrar for a period of ten years from 1976-77 to 1985-86 (**Table 5.1**). A comparison of the land values in the years 1976-77 and 1985-86 showed that while the average values for the city as a whole increased by 300 per cent, for individual localities the increase varied from about 100 to about 1200 per cent.[1] The land values in the sample localities were further analysed using the yearly average values for all the ten years. A linear time trend of the following type :

$$Vt = a + bt,$$

where *Vt* is land value for the year *t*,

t varying from 1 to 10, and *a* and *b* are constants.

was fitted to the yearly averages for each locality (**Table 5.2 Fig 5.1**).

TABLE 5.1 : **Land value in rupees for 1 Sq. ft. area in Bangalore City and in different localities (1976-77 to 1985-86)**

(Rs./sq. ft.)

Locality	*1976-77*	*1977-78*	*1978-79*	*1979-80*	*1980-81*	*1981-82*	*1982-83*	*1983-84*	*1984-85*	*1985-86*
Gandhinagar	88.68	45.44	83.13	40.81	98.73	116.68	108.81	205.10	181.23	171.16
Chamarajpet	20.21	27.20	27.08	25.41	29.70	45.38	51.32	48.88	66.80	95.17
Srirampuram	4.17	12.89	33.90	16.83	15.22	19.79	20.42	23.42	28.42	67.65
Wilson Garden	17.88	20.24	29.18	21.81	31.50	25.77	44.13	78.67	84.07	104.20
Frazer Town	20.74	20.06	14.63	13.52	15.44	22.91	29.85	35.06	47.35	87.20
Malleswaram	17.16	15.75	15.29	11.89	86.35	30.81	37.60	43.05	54.04	124.09
HAL II Stage	23.33	15.63	12.50	11.41	22.44	26.92	41.06	45.44	52.54	65.08
Rajajinagar	25.42	18.64	27.92	14.99	23.99	33.39	52.76	63.88	61.06	91.74
Jayanagar	22.23	12.43	16.59	19.44	31.29	31.28	39.34	44.56	64.29	86.19
Koramangala	—	9.42	3.17	4.84	14.80	18.29	47.52	37.57	43.27	56.32
Sadashivnagar	8.58	18.84	56.22	23.52	15.97	16.29	43.46	27.14	37.86	109.67
Bangalore City	24.84	19.69	29.06	18.59	35.03	35.24	46.93	59.34	65.54	96.23

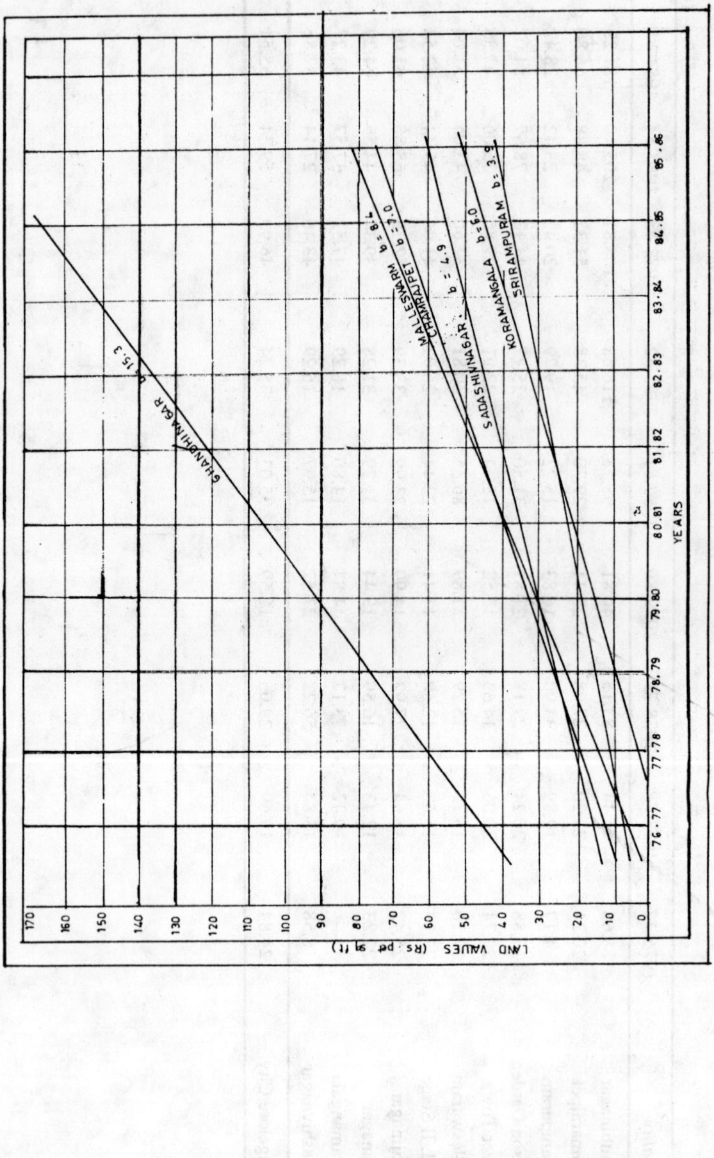

Fig. 5.1 : Time Trends of Land values in selected localities in Bangalore

TABLE 5.2 : **Time Trend in Land Values in Bangalore City 1976-77 to 1985-86 (*Vt* = *a* + *bt*)**

Locality	*Time Trend Land Values*	*Correlation coefficient*
Gandhinagar	15.30	0.83
Chamarajpet	6.99	0.91
Sriramapuram	3.90	0.68
Wilson Garden	9.29	0.90
Frazer Town	4.01	0.61
Nalleswaram	8.43	0.70
HAL II Stage	5.41	0.89
Rajajinagar	7.25	0.88
Jayanagar	7.23	0.87
Koramangala	6.00	0.91
Sadeshivnagar	4.89	0.54
Bangalore City	7.27	0.90

The rates of increases in land values (*b*) was found to be the highest in Gandhinagar locality, followed by Wilson Garden, Malleswaram, HAL II stage, Sadashivanagar, Frazer Town and Srirampuram. The localities in the central part of the city and those of high socio-economic status showed higher rates of increase in land values during the ten-year period. while peripheral and low status localities showed relatively lower rates of increase. The level of land values also varied in different parts of the city. Localities in the city core had high land values which, on the whole, declined with distance from the city core.

The rate of increase in land prices was also studied with reference to the base years 1950-51, 1960-61 and 1970-71. With reference to these base years, the rise in price level for Bangalore City was phenomenally high — 4,215 per cent compared to 1950-51, 2,159 per cent compared to 1960-61 and 1,257 per cent compared to 1970-71 (**Table 5.3**). It needs to be clarified that the data for 1950-51 relates to three localities, for 1960-61 to six localities and for 1970-71 to eight localities.

It must be mentioned here that the values as recorded in the Sub-Registrar's office may not be the same as the actual values of the transaction. It is common knowledge that the registered values are often reported as lower than the actual values. Nevertheless, the above analysis clearly brings out the upward trend in land values in the city and the variations in the trend associated with locational and socio-economic characteristics.

TABLE 5.3 : **Annual Land value and Percentage Increase per Sq. ft. in Bangalore City and Different Localities (1950-51 to 1985-86)**

(rupees at current price)

Localtiy	*1950-51*	*1960-61*	*1970-71*	*1975-76*	*1980-81*	*1985-86*	*Percentage increase* From the base year	*Percentage increase* From 1975-77 to 1985-86
1	2	3	4	5	6	7	8	9
Gandhinagar	-	12.31	15.95	56.05	98.73	177.16	1,290.4+	205.30
Chanarajpet	2.76	2.63	8.48	21.80	29.70	95.17	3,348.2*	336.60
Srirampuram	-	-	2.92	5.22	15.12	67.65	2,216.8#	1,195.90
Wilson Garden	1.18	2.31	9.66	15.19	31.50	104.20	8,730.5*	595.90
Frazer Town	-	1.20	4.87	14.88	15.44	87.20	7,166.7+	486.00
Malleswaram	2.76	5.77	8.97	21.35	86.35	124.90	4,396*	481.20
HAL II Stage	-	-	-	10.33	22.44	65.80	-	530.00
Rajajinagar	-	-	-	22.55	23.99	91.74	-	306.80
Jayanagar	-	-	-	15.60	31.29	86.19	-	452.50
Koramangala	-	0.34	1.39	2.74	14.80	56.32	12,464.7+	1,955.40
Sadashivnagar	-	-	4.45	8.60	15.97	109.67	2,364.5#	1,175.20
Bangalore City	2.23	4.26	7.90	17.66	35.30	96.23	4,215.2*	444.90

* Base Year 1950-51
\+ Base Year 1960-61
\# Base Year 1970-71

Land Prices of BDA Sites

Allotment Price : **Table 5.4** shows the rates at which the BDA has allotted sites to the general public. These sites were formed in new layouts/extensions and were located at the periphery of the city at the time of formation. The price charged by BDA has shown a steady rise over a period of 10-12 years. A site measuring 30′ × 40′ meant for the low income groups which was sold at Rs. 3 to Rs. 4 per sq. ft. in 1975 was raised to 6.67 per sq.ft in 1982 and to Rs. 7.25 per sq.ft in 1984, an increase of 80 to 100 per cent in 9 years. The rate was further jacked up to Rs. 16.72 per sq.ft in 1986 and to Rs.20.82 in 1987. Thus the prices went up by more than 500 per cent in a period of 12 years.

It is interesting to note that the rates in respect of the sites of higher dimensions *i.e.* 40′ × 60′ and 50′ × 80′ have also registered increases ranging from 5 to 6 times during the same period of 12 years. It is strange that the price differential between smaller and bigger sites has narrowed down and there is little difference in rates of sites measuring 30′× 40′, 40′ × 60′ and 50′ × 80′ in 1987.

TABLE 5.4 (i) **Price of Sites allotted by Banglore Development Authority, 1975**

Year	*20 × 30*	*30 × 40*	*40 × 60*	*50 × 80*	*60 × 90*
1975	1.55 to 2.00	3.00 to 4.00	3.50 to 4.55	4.75 to 5.10	4.45 to 5.20
1982	—	6.65	7.75	8.20	10.00
February 1984	—	7.25	9.75	110.40	12.55
October 1984	—	12.55	16.70	10.75	—
March 1986	8.33	12.55 to 20.90	16.70 to 20.90	—	—
December 1986	8.35	16.70	20.90	21.25	—
1987	10.00	20.85	22.90	22.50	—

Localities covered are : HAL II Stage, Koramangala, Sarakki, Banashankari II & III Stage, Hoshalli, RPC Layout, West of Chord Road, Rajamahal Vilas Extension, BTM Layout, Hennur Road-Banasavadi Road, Agara (Hosur Road- Sarjopur Rd.,) Old Madras Road, NGEF East.

Auction Price : A true indication of the market price can be had from the rates obtained by auction of certain sites by BDA. The Rules prescribe that commercial sites and corner residential sites in any layout be sold in public auction. **Table 5.5** shows the average auction rates in respect of such sites. The data cover the period from 1984-85 to 1987-88

TABLE 5.4 (ii) : **Prices of Sites allotted by Bangalore Development Authority, 1975**

(Rs./aq. ft.)

Name of the Layout	*20×30*	*30×40*	*30×50*	*45×60*	*30×45*	*40×60*	*50×80*	*60×90*
1	*2*	*3*	*4*	*5*	*6*	*7*	*8*	*9*
HAL II Stage	2.00	4.00	4.50	4.55	4.55	4.55	5.10	5.10
Koramangala	2.00	4.00	4.10	4.10	4.10	4.10	4.70	4.70
Sarakki	1.90	3.80	4.25	4.25	4.25	4.25	4.55	4.55
Banashankari II Stage	1.55	3.10	3.35	3.35	3.35	3.35	4.00	4.00
Banashankari III Stage	1.55	3.10	3.35	3.35	3.35	3.35	4.00	4.00
MRC Road	1.85	3.70	4.35	4.35	4.35	4.35	4.75	4.75
Hosahalli	1.85	3.70	4.35	4.35	4.35	4.35	4.75	4.75
RPC Layout	1.65	3.35	4.00	4.00	4.00	4.00	4.45	4.45
West of Chord Road	2.00	4.00	4.55	4.55	4.55	4.55	4.75	5.20
Rajmehal Vilas	-	-	-	8.90	8.90	8.90	11.10	11.10

for ten localities. These localities have been chosen as auctions were held by BDA for the sites in these layouts during that period. The price level for residential sites has ranged from Rs. 100 to Rs.133 per sq.ft. For commercial sites, the rates obtained varied from Rs. 112 to Rs. 152 per sq.ft. Only in Gangenahally, a very high rate of Rs. 200 per sq.ft has obtained for the year 1987-88. The variations in the price level during the last 4 years is not significant. Sometimes, a decline is seen in the price in the same locality. For instance, in Banashankari II stage, the rate for commercial sites was Rs. 153 in 1984-85, Rs. 126 in 1985-86 and Rs. 111 in the year 1987-88. Mattadahally layout has shown a considerable increase between 1986-87 (Rs. 91 per sq.ft) and 1987-88 (Rs. 120 per sq.ft). Auction rates also depend on certain factors like exact location of the site (locational advantage of the site like proximity to the main road etc.,) and the competition at the time of bidding.

TABLE 5.5 : **Average Auction Prices of Commercial and Residential BDA Sites**

(Rs./sq. ft.)

Name of the Area	*Commercial Sites*				*Residential Sites*			
	1984-85	*1985-86*	*1986-87*	*1987-87*	*1984-85*	*1985-86*	*1986-87*	*1987-88*
Banashankari II Stage	152.65	126.60	—	111.50	—	—	—	—
HAL II Stage	—	—	122.80	—	131.75	105.00	—	—
Koramangala	—	—	119.85	—	—	92.90	--	110.35
Sarakati	—	—	—	139.35	—		—	119.85
Rabindranath Tagore Nagar	—	—	—	—	—	—	102.55	—
Hennur Road	—	—	—	—	—	—	47.10	—
Pillamna Gdn	—	—	—	—	—	104.15	110.25	—
Gangenahalli	—	—	—	199.90	—	—	—	—
Matadahalli	—	—	91.50	118.65	—	—	—	—
Mahalakashmi Layout	—	—	—	—	—	—	100.90	—
West of Chord Road	—	—	—	—	118.00	—	—	133.30

The price obtained in the case of commercial use of land is not significantly higher than that of residential use as one would have expected. One reason could be that the locations are in new areas in the periphery of the city, far away from the city centre and where it would take sometime for business to pick up. As Northam has argued, the willingness to buy locations away from the point of greatest desirability gradually diminishes and the bid rent curve for commercial use gradually slopes downward. On the other hand, the relatively high price fetched for residential use indicates that such locations may be desirable for residential purposes thus confirming Northam's hypothesis that the value of residential land is determined less by the bid rent curve than by the indifference curve, *i.e.,* residential land users are indifferent to distance from the best location, atleast to a degree.

Prices for Other Purposes : The BDA also allots sites for certain purposes other than housing and commercial—for civic amenities, *kalyana mantaps,* industries etc. The rates for different purposes are as follows:

(a) civic amenity sites for religious and charitable purposes and certain public institutions—50 per cent of the ruling allotment rate of residential sites;
(b) for Kalyana Mantapa (halls for celebration of marriages)—twice the ruling allotment rate;
(c) for private institutions other than Kalyana Mantaps—prevailing allotment rate;
(d) for industrial sites—Rs. 1.50 to Rs. 2.30 per sq.ft till 1984 and Rs. 10.45 per sq.ft. since 1984.

Sites are allotted at concessional rates for religious and charitable purposes. Although the rate for Kalyana Mantaps is twice the allotment rate, it is to be noted that Kalyana Mantaps are actually used on commercial basis and the allotment rate of BDA must be treated as very low. Even for industrial sites, it must be stated that rates till 1984 were on a concessional basis.

Land Value fixed by State Government

The Revenue Department of the State Government had from time to time, fixed the maximum land values for different localities in the city for the purpose of valuation of properties. These values were expected to guide the Sub-Registrar at the time of registering private transactions. The values so fixed in 1975, 1982 and 1985 for 11 localities in the city are given in Table 5.6. The revision made in 1985 was quite steep compared to the values fixed in 1982. The valuation went up from Rs. 6 to Rs. 55 per sq.ft in Jayanagar 9th Block, from Rs. 14 to Rs. 167 per sq.ft in Palace Orchards and from Rs. 8 to Rs. 200 per sq.ft in Gandhinagar. Registration could be refused if sales were sought to be made below these values. The notification issued by Government fixing these land values has been struck down by the High Court as invalid. Nevertheless, it serves to highlight the land values in the city as determined by the Government.

TABLE 5.6 : **Land Values in the City of Bangalore (Fixed by the Revenue Department)**

(Rs./sq. ft.)

Name of locality	*1975*	*1982*	*1985*
Maeleswaram Area	11.60	23.20	100.00
CITB Layout, *i.e.*, Rajajinagar I Stage	7.90	15.80	88.90
Chamarajpet	11.60	23.20	100.00
Jayanagar I, II, III & IV Block	7.90	15.80	83.35
Jayanagar V, VI, VII & VIII Blocks	6.50	13.00	72.20
Wilson Garden	7.90	15.80	88.90
Palace Orchards	13.95	27.90	166.65
Gandhinagar	7.90	15.80	200.00
Indiranagar, HAL Layout & Domlur	6.50	13.00	83.55
Jayanagar IX Block	6.00	12.05	55.55
Frazer Town	6.50	13.00	77.75

Source : Revenue Department, Government of Karnataka.

Land Price Estimates by Real Estate Agents

From the information collected informally from Real Estate Agents and private developers in the city, it would appear that in the time period of 15 years (1973 to 1987), the value of land in Bangalore City had increased by 20 times and between 1980 and 1987 by about 10 times. Estimated land prices in the selected shopping and residential localities and at different distance intervals from the city centre based on the information are given in **Tables 5.7 and 5.8**. The most fashionable shopping area in the city core, *viz.* Mahatma Gandhi Road had the highest land value — Rs.350 to Rs. 500 per sq.ft, while the developing peripheral residential areas such as Koramangala had land values ranging from Rs. 80 to Rs. 150 per sq.ft.

Compared to the registered price of land transaction the price gathered from the estate agents showed a variation ranging from 20 per cent (Wilson Gardens) to 150 per cent (Jayanagar) in about the same year (1986-87). While the average land values within one km from the city centre (Vidhana Soudha) were estimated at about Rs. 320 per sq.ft, the same were about Rs. 95 per sq.ft at peripheral locations. The value for land plots (revenue sites) just outside the city periphery, at a distance of 12 kms from city centre were Rs. 40 per sq.ft which declined to Rs. 20 per sq.ft at a distance of 15 kms from the city

TABLE 5.7 : **Estimated Land Values in Selected Areas based on discussions with Real Estate Agents**

(Rs./sq. ft).

Locality	*Land Price range in 1987*
Around MG Road	350—500
Cox Town	120—150
Jayanagar	180—250
Palace Orchards, Basavanagudi	200—300
Wilson Garden	120—150
Koramangala	80—150
BDA Layouts (Peripheral) Auction	75—120
Allotment	18—25
Revenue Land (Agricultural)	10—40
Yelahank	10—20
Hosur	6—10

Increase in land values from 1973 to 1987 — about 20 times.
Increase in land values from 1980 to 1987 — about 10 times.

centre (Table 5.8). The pattern of decline in land values with distance from the city centre was of the negative exponential form (*Vd* = 388.34 e-0.1916d, where *Vd* is land value at distance *d* and *e* is the base of natural logarithms; the correlation coefficient of the 'fit' was —0.996). The scatter diagram of land values of different average distances clearly brought out three zones showing significant differences in gradient patterns: (i) the first zone of sharp decline up to 4 km. from city centre; (ii) the second zone of average decline for 4 km. to 8 km, and (iii) the third zone of moderate decline for 9 km to 15 km. (**Fig. 5.2**).

TABLE 5.8 : **Estimated land values in Bangalore city with distance from City Centre, based on discussion with Real Estate agents**

(Rs./sq. ft.)

Average distance from city centre (Vidhana Soudha) (in kms.)	*Land Value in 1987*
1.0	320
2.0	260
3.0	215
4.0	160
5.0	155
6.0	120
7.0	110
8.0	95
12.0	40
15.0	20

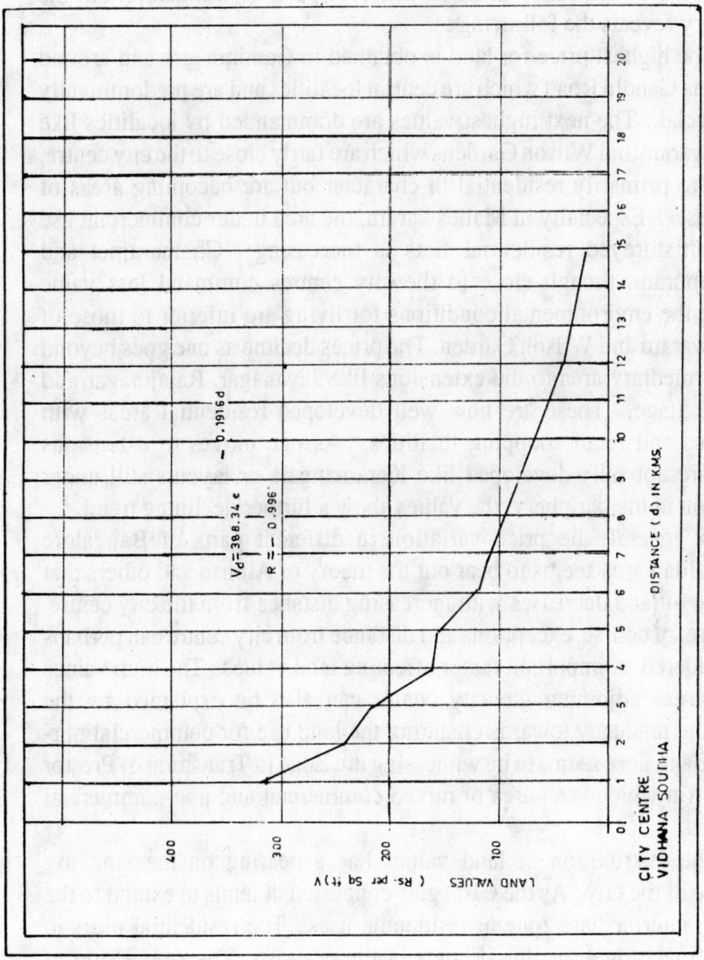

Fig. 5.2 : Land values decline with distance from city centre

Spatial Distribution of Land Values

An analysis of the land values in different parts of Bangalore and the periphery reveals the following :

The highest price for land is obtained in Gandhinagar and around Mahatma Gandhi Road which are central localities and are predominantly commercial. The next highest values are commanded by localities like Malleswaram and Wilson Gardens which are fairly close to the city centre. These are primarily residential in character but are becoming areas of mixed uses. Especially in Malleswaram, the area under commercial use and multistoreyed residential flats is increasing. Chamarajpet and Sriramapuram, though close to the city centres command less value because the environmental conditions for living are inferior to those of Malleswaram and Wilson Garden. The prices decline as one goes beyond the intermediary area to the extensions like Jayanagar, Rajajinagar and HAL II Stage. These are now well developed residential areas with amenities and retail shopping facilities. As one moves to extensions which are not fully developed like Koramangala or layouts still under formation in the periphery, the values show a further declining trend.

In general, the price variation in different parts of Bangalore metropolitan area seems to bear out the theory of Alonso and others that the price of land decreases with increasing distance from the city centre. There are, of course, exceptions and distance from city centre can perhaps be considered an important factor affecting land values. The high values in the areas adjoining the city centre can also be explained by the increasing tendency towards changing the land use for commercial purposes. Bangalore seems to be witnessing the Zone in Transition of Prestor and Griffin which is an area of mixed commercial and non-commercial land uses.

The distribution of land values has a bearing on the land use structure of the city. As the CBD gets congested, it tends to extend to the adjacent intermediate zone of residential uses. The residential users in turn encroach on agricultural lands in the outskirts. The conversion of agricultural lands in the fringe areas of Bangalore for establishing residential colonies is a manifestation of this phenomenon. Another consequence of physical expansion is the more intensive use of land in the core and adjacent areas of the city as is evidenced by high-rise buildings both for commercial and residential purposes. This also indicates the preference for 'nearness'—the theory enunciated by Hurd—atleast on the part of some people. This again tends to push up land values within the city.

An interesting case with regard to central areas, particularly the CBD is the old part of the city which does not experience the desired change as expected from the theory of bid rents. Although the land values in these areas are very high, because of the low rental values of the premises protected by the Rent Control Act, the occupants of these buildings are not willing to shift to intermediate and peripheral locations. The owners therefore are not willing to make any improvements and the old building stock slowly deteriorates. This is the situation in old areas of Bangalore like Avenue Road, Chickpet, Shivajinagar, etc.

The low price level in the periphery of the rural-urban fringe of Bangalore has promoted speculative activity. Real estate speculators purchase land (especially agricultural or unconverted land which is cheap), in anticipation of rise in land values and hold them for earning profits at a future date. This in a way is related to the role of public authorities which permits conversion of agricultural land for urban uses as also the weak enforcement of the restrictions on transfer of agricultural land or on changing its use.

From the foregoing analysis of the price trends of urban land in Bangalore, the following conclusions can be drawn:

(a) No credible record of land prices is available. The sources from which prices are obtained, *viz.*, the registered price given in the sale deeds and the prices of allotment or auction by BDA do not present a correct picture of the price prevailing in the land market. There is gross undervaluation of land in order to evade registration fees and other taxes. The allotment price of BDA is artificially pegged low to subsidise the weaker sections and the auction price may be said to reflect a strong element of scarcity value as land is put on the market in very small parcels. The prices obtained from Real Estate agents may reflect the market value with greater authenticity.

(b) Land prices have shown a continuously rising trend in space and time. While the prices in the city centre have continued to be high compared to other areas, the rate of increase has been higher in the newly developed extensions of BDA. Residential land prices are affected more by environmental factors like social status of neighbours and aesthetic surroundings than by central location.

(c) Land in commercial areas commands a higher value than in residential areas (*eg*. MG Road, Gandhinagar) bearing out the dictum that there is a 'permanent distance' between commercial and residential land prices.

GOVERNMENT INTERVENTION IN THE LAND MARKET

Land values reflect the interaction of a number of macro-level forces like city size, population growth and socio-economic development, apart from factors directly relevant to the land market like land use, location, accessibility and so on. The important factors which have contributed to the dramatic increase in the land values in Bangalore at the macro-level are the following:

(a) the rapid growth in population, especially during the decade 1971-81 (76%) resulting in increased demand for land;

(b) economic development of the city on account of industrialisation and expansion in teritary sector. This has brought about increase in the income of the population. There is a growing trend to invest surplus funds, particularly black money, in real estate.

(c) Social trends—owning a house (as big and as fashionable as possible) has become a status symbol among all sections of the population in Bangalore, except the poor. People are, therefore, willing to pay a high price for land. They also consider it a good investment.

The above matters relate to larger issues of national economy and the social forces of development. They, however, serve to highlight the complicated task of controlling the prices of land. Some attempts made by the Government to regulate land price in Bangalore are the following:

Public Acquisition of Land

Compulsory acquisition of land from private land owners is one of the means of capturing the unearned increments from the value of land. The land thus acquired is used for public purposes and also to provide housing and other amenities to the public at large. Although a fairly large number of house sites have been made available in Bangalore through this method, it has not had any direct effect on the market value of the land.

Restricting Ownership Rights

The Urban Land Ceiling and Regulation Act, 1976, imposes a ceiling limit on the extent of vacant land a person can hold in an urban agglomeration. The excess land is to be taken over by the government at a value far below the market price and utilised for housing and other public purposes. However, very little land in excess of the limit has been acquired in Bangalore and this has not in any way influenced the land price level.

Right of Preemption

The Urban Ceiling Law also provides the first option to government to buy vacant land, whenever, it is sold. In other words, Government can enter the land market as a buyer, whenever, there is a sale transaction. This is expected to curb speculation. But this preemptive right has hardly been exercised by government and speculative activity as well as profiteering in land are thriving in the city.

While the first measure, namely, public acquisition of land has been resorted to on a fairly large scale in Bangalore, the other two measures under the Urban Land Ceiling Laws have not been implemented in the right spirit. On the whole, none of these measures has really helped in controlling land prices in Bangalore.

Impact of Changes in Land use

Land use and land use changes play a vital role in determining land prices. Strangely, this is one area where the decisions of public authorities contribute to a rise in land values. The change of land use from agricultural to urban and from residential to commercial—results in creation of additional land value almost instantaneously. While the change in value is created by a decision of the public authority, the additional value is actually collected by the land owner. It may be added that some of the changes in land use take place in Bangalore without the permission of the Planning Authority, *i.e.,* illegally, thus contributing to distortions in planning.

The various theories of land values become relevant mainly with reference to a free market economy where a particular piece of land is put to a particular use with a view to maximising profit. In spite of several legal restrictions on the transfer or use of land, land values in Bangalore have shown a rising trend as most of urban land is in private hands. The phenomenon has encouraged the tendency to convert land for profitable uses legally or illegally.

The intervention of public authorities like Bangalore Development Authority in the land market, while making available house plots to a limited number of people, has not had the effect of controlling land prices. In fact, certain adverse consequences have flowed from the low prices offered by BDA for its land. Some beneficiaries of BDA allocation have indulged in speculative activity thus pushing publicly acquired and distributed land into the market. There are also instances of the poor selling the land allotted to them for, whatever, profit they might get and continuing to live in slums. Based on this experience in Bangalore which is common to other Indian cities, a hypothesis can be postulated thus: Where the disparity between the price of land in the market and that offered by a public authority is very wide and the quantity of land supplied by the public authority is small, the market price will continue to be high.

NOTES

1. The Consumer Price Index for Bangalore increased by 239 per cent between 1970-71 and 1985-86 (from 172 to 583 with base year 1960), while the land value shot up by 1,257 per cent during the same period. Thus, even if the land values are corrected for inflation, their rise must be considered very steep.
2. The prices are shown locality-wise for 1975 in **Table 5.4(i)**. Subsequently, only prices have been given, whenever, revision has taken place in **Table 5.4 (ii)**.
3. One of the estate agents reported a land transaction in which a bit of land in Mahatma Gandhi Road was sold for Rs. 1,200 per sq. ft. in the year 1987.

6

LAND USE PLANNING IN BANGALORE

THE PLANNING PROCESS

Objectives of Planning

Policy states what needs to be accomplished and planning deals with the ways of doing it (Northam, 1975). Urban Land Policy sets goals and objectives in relation to the manner in which urban land is to be used. The planning process explores the mechanism of implementing the policy or realising the goals and objectives. Within the planning process, the preparation of a specific plan for the use and development of urban land is dependent on a variety of policy decisions. Urban land use policies give direction to the urban planning process on the one hand, and become conditioned by the findings derived from the planning process on the other.

Urban planning deals with spatial development of urban settlements, which involves the use and development of land. As urban land is a scarce resource and it is required for location of various activities in which people are engaged, the regulation of the use and development of land has a profound effect on economic and social issues. Physical growth must be planned to suit the social and economic needs of the people. Land Use Planning must, therefore, be concerned with not only the specifics of land use patterns but the functional requirements of the individual city. For a metropolitan city like Bangalore, planning has to deal with issues like migration, housing for the growing population, public transportation, educational and health facilities and employment. Formulation of policies to achieve social objectives involving the utilisation of all available resources is one of the tasks of Urban Planning and a Land Use Plan must serve as an instrument to implement such policies.

In order to achieve the planning goals of reconciling the competing claims of limited land and providing a physical environment conducive to better community life, it is necessary for government to regulate and control the use of land. Hence, the need for planning the use of land. The specific objectives of Land Use Planning may be stated as follows :

(i) to provide public amenities like roads, utilities and open space which are not likely to be produced by private initiative;
(ii) to increase efficiency in land use by prescribing standards for development; and
(iii) to ensure that the benefits of development accrue to the community as a whole.

The means or techniques used to achieve the above objectives fall into two categories :

(a) direct intervention by government to organize land uses more effectively — this can be done by acquiring land, providing infrastructure and services to facilitate development or, by directly financing development.
(b) restricting or directing Private Land Use and Development — this is usually done by zoning, subdivision and building controls.

This chapter focuses mainly on the second category and discusses the nature and efficacy of Land Use Controls including the Master Plan used as part of the planning process in Bangalore.

Legal Framework and Plan Preparation

Any Land Use Policy for Bangalore has to operate within the legal framework of the Karnataka Town and Country Planning Act which came into force on 15th January 1965. The key elements in the formulation of such policy would be the following :

(i) Declaration of a Local Planning Area.
(ii) Constitution of a Planning Authority for the Planning Area.
(iii) Preparation of Development Plan (including Land Use Plan).

As required under Section 1(a) of the KTCP Act, the Bangalore Local Planning Area was declared by the State Government in December 1966. In accordance with Section 4(c) of the same Act, Bangalore City Planning Authority was constituted on 8th August, 1967 for the Bangalore City Planning Area. Under the law, the following stages are envisaged in planning:

(i) To start with, an Outline Development Plan has to be prepared indicating generally the manner in which the development and improvement of the planning area is to be carried out. The object of this outline or interim plan is to afford some guidance in regulating the use and development of undeveloped areas and vacant plots in built-up areas, until a more comprehensive plan is ready to replace it. It is essentially a short-term instrument of controlling land use. The ODP shall include a general Land Use Plan and Zoning of Land Use for residential, commercial, industrial, agricultural, recreational, educational and other purposes.

(ii) The making of Comprehensive Development Plan (CDP) constitutes the second stage. During this stage, the preliminary surveys made in the earlier stage are supplemented by detailed investigations and the long-term needs and potentialities of the area are formulated in detail. The Comprehensive Development Plan is intended o serve as a standing blue print of the land uses to be permitted, and the developments and improvements to be made in the entire planning area over a fairly long period. It shall include proposals for comprehensive zoning of land use for the planning area, together with zoning regulations, new areas earmarked for future development and expansion and the stages by which the plan has to be carried out.

The proposals shall also deal with the following aspects :

(a) acquisition of land for the purpose of implementing the plan;
(b) financial responsibility connected with the proposed improvements; and
(c) the manner in which these responsibilities are proposed to be met.

Both in the case of ODP and CDP, the procedure of publishing the plan and inviting public comments is to be followed. Thereafter the plan is submitted to government for its final approval.

(iii) The third stage comprises the preparation of detailed town improvement schemes for the purpose of implementing the proposals contained in the CP. Such schemes may provide for laying out of new streets, improvement of roads and communications, constructions, alteration and removal of buildings and other structures, allotment and reservation of land for roads, open spaces, gardens, markets, green belts, lighting, water supply, drainage and the preservation of objects and buildings of historical or national interest. The Act provides for meeting the costs of a Town Planning Scheme by contribution from the owner of each plot included in the scheme.

PLANNING AND CHANGES IN LAND USE PATTERN : 1961-83

One of the first tasks of planning is to allocate the land available in the Local Planning Area for different uses. The Planning Area has been broadly divided into two categories—the 'conurbation area,' *i.e.,* the area delineated for the purpose of development and the 'Green Belt' (CDP) or 'Rural Tract' (ODP) where no developments are to take place and which should retain its rural or green character. The ODP covered a total planning area of 500 sq. km. of which an extent of 265 sq.km constituted the conurbation area and the remaining 235 sq. km. the rural tract. The CDP provided for an Enlarged Planning Area of 1,279 sq. km. of which the conurbation area would cover 439.28 sq. km. and the balance extent of 839 sq. km. would serve as the green belt.

The land use classification adopted for Bangalore is as follows:

(a) Residential;
(b) Commercial;
(c) Open spaces, parks, playgrounds and recreational area;
(e) Public and semi-public use;
(f) Transport and communication;
(g) Agricultural land (green belt); and
(h) Defence land (unclassified).

A survey of the existing land uses was made before preparation of the plans. Such surveys were made in 1961 and 1972 at the time of preparing the ODP and again in 1983 while preparing the CDP. Particulars of different land uses prevailing at these points of time are given in **Table 6.1**. The land uses proposed for the year 1976 is shown in **Table 6.2**. An analysis of these uses reveals that while the total area under different land uses increased by 7,120 acres between 1961 and 1972, the increase registered between 1972 and 1983 was 15,585 acres. Thus, the decade 1972-83 witnessed an expansion in the Land Use Area more than twice compared to the decade 1961-72. It is interesting to note that the population growth in these two decades also registered a similar increase.

While the population during 1961-71 increased by 38 per cent, the increase during 1971-81 was 76 per cent.

TABLE 6.1 : **Land Uses—Existing (1961, 1972 and 1983)**

Classification	*1961*		*1972*		*1983*	
	Area (acres)	*%age of Total Area*	*Area (acres)*	*%age of Total Area*	*Area (acres)*	*%age of Total Area*
Residential	10,528	37.50	14,537	41.34	14,271	28.40
Commercial	683	2.55	958	2.73	1,566	3.13
Industrial	3,069	10.57	3,069	8.74	4,833	9.65
Public and Semi-Public buildings	2,100	7.60	2,596	7.40	6,258	12.49
Parks, Playgrounds and Recreational areas	2,206	7.98	2,485	7.08	5,064	10.11
Agricultural	2,940	10.60	2,940	8.37	—	—
Defence Land	6,474	23.20	7,179	20.43	5,222	10.42
Transport (Railways and Airport)	—	—	1,356	3.86	12,886	27.72
Total	28,000	100.00	3,5120	100.00	50,100	100.00

Sources : Outline Devlopment Plan 1972.
Comprhensive Devlopment Plan, 1984.

TABLE 6.2 : **Land Uses Proposed (1976) — Bangalore Metropolitan Area**

Classification	*Proposed (1976)*
Residential	27,845
Commercial	2,219
Industrial	12,483
Public and Semi-public	4,513
Parks, Playgrounds and recreational areas	6,443
Agricultural	2,604
Defence land	6,641
Transport (Railways, Airport)	2,604
Total	65,357

Source : Outline Development Plan, 1972.

Between 1961 and 1983, the developed area of the city increased by 22,100 acres or 80 per cent. Proportionately, the area under residential use declined from 37.5 per cent of the total area to 28.5 per cent. It needs to be explained that in 1961 (and also in 1972) roads and streets were included under residential use, whereas, in 1983, they were excluded. It is estimated that roads and streets generally constitute about 20 to 25 per cent of the residential area. Even if this is taken into account, the proportion of residential use would go up to 30 per cent. The actual area used for residential purpose went up to 14,270 acres (or about 17,800 acres if roads are included), far short of 27,845 acres or 43 per cent of the total area the planners had envisaged.

The proportion of land under industrial use also showed a slight decline from 10.6 to 9.6 per cent. The area proposed for industrial development in the ODP (1972) was to the extent of 12,483 acres by 1976 whereas, the actual utilisation was only 4,833 acres even by 1983, *i.e.* just about 35 per cent. This is a surprising shortfall considering the conscious decision of the planners to earmark a substantial area for industrial development and also the enthusiasm shown by the industrialists, as is evident from what was stated in the plan; "When the Outline Development Plan which was provisionally approved by Government, a number of people and public institutions like Chamber of Commerce, Institute of Engineers represented that the area reserved for industry within the ODP is highly inadequate and requested to reserve another 6,000 acres more, over and above 6,408 acres provided in the ODP. Therefore, a provision is now made to earmark more industrial ares."

The area under commercial use went up by 883 acres, the proportion showing a marginal rise of 2.5 per cent to 31 per cent. Here also, the use has not increased to the expected extent of 2,219 acres. The land under public and semi-public use registered a considerable increase of nearly three times and its proportion to total use went up from 7.6 per cent to 12.5 per cent. The land used for parks, playgrounds and recreational areas more than doubled, although it fell short of the area proposed in the plan by about 1400 acres. (**Table 6.3**)

TABLE 6.3 : **Land Uses Proposed (2001) Bangalore Metropolitan Area**

Classification	*Proposed (2001)*
Residential	43,472
Commercial	4,126
Industrial	7,375
Public and semi-public	9,296
Parks, playgrounds and open spaces	14,772
Transport	24,018
Unclassified	5,493
	1,08,502

Note : Transportation Zone includes the roads and streets of other land use zones.
Source : Comprehensive Development Plan, 1984.

The biggest rise was recorded in the land use pertaining to transport — 11,529 acres, nearly ten times the area that prevailed in 1972. Even as a proportion of the total land use area, it registered a steep increase, from less than 4 per cent to nearly 28 per cent. This tremendous change in transportation use is explained by the fact that in 1972, the land use under transport included only the area covered by railway and airports, but not streets and roads. In 1983, the area under transport covered not only the land under railways and airport but also roads and streets. Even so, the increase under this use must be considered significant.

It is not possible to assess the change in the area under agricultural use as the CDP has excluded agriculture from its land use profile. No change is noticed in the area under agriculture between 1961 and 1972, although the proportion of agricultural land declined from 10.6 per cent to 8.3 per cent. In fact, the ODP recognised the difficulty in preserving the rural features in the villages adjoining the city and suggested positive measures for promotion of agriculture : "An intensive effort must be made by the State Departments concerned to encourage cultivation of grapes, fruits, vegetables and other high-priced produce and rural industries such as dairying and poultry rearing. It is desirable to undertake social forestry on the less fertile lands to supply a part of the needs of the city for domestic fuel and preserve the suburban landscape". It is observed from actual developments that, far from strict regulation of building activity, unauthorised constructions have come up encroaching agricultural lands.

The Defence authorities still occupy a considerable extent of land in the city (5,222) acres although the total area under their control has declined by 1,250 acres. The ODP has made some perceptive observations on Defence lands : "The defence authorities are in possession of large areas of lands scattered throughout the city from the north-west to the southeast. In addition, they hold extensive blocks of land outside the municipal limits. By notifications issued in 1949, lands lying within the Corporation boundaries under the control of the defence authorities were excluded from the jurisdiction of the Corporation, thus creating an imperium, so to speak in Bangalore. The area of the land so excluded is about 5 sq. miles (12.5 sq.km.). It is suggested that the State Government should be requested to move in this matter and persuade the defence authorities to vacate the lands and buildings held by them in the city limits and establish a cantonment nearby in the Metropolitan Rural Area, where all their activities can be concentrated." This suggestion has obviously not been implemented and the defence authorities continue to occupy lands in different parts of the city, even in the most central areas like M.G. Road.

It is, however, interesting to note that the CDP without dwelling on the question of defence land, has made a cryptic remark thus: "In a way, these defence areas which are sparsely developed act also as lung spaces and in some cases they form barriers segregating the areas on either side of such large defence uses."

On the whole, the plan to utilise 65,357 acres of land by 1976 did not materialise. Even by 1983, the utilisation was only to the extent of 50,100 acres—a shortfall of 15,257 acres.

The Land Use Plan contemplated for the year 1976 given in **Fig. 6.2** and the land uses actually existing in 1983 shown in **Fig. 6.1** reveal that the city did not grow as planned. A considerable area proposed for residential use, particularly in and around central areas has been put to commercial use. Industrial development did not take place to the extent planned in different directions along Tumkur Road, Bellary Road, Whitefield Road (towards Madras), Hosur Road and Mysore Road. The utilisation of land for industrial use was only 35 per cent of what was planned early by 1983. Residential development proposed along Hosur Road, to the north and south of Old Madras Road and to the south of Tumkur Road did not come up as expected. Another feature of the land use pattern in 1983 is the scattered developments outside the conurbation area or in the area earmarked as green belt. Such developments existed earlier as seen in **Fig. 6.2.** What is obvious is the growth of unplanned land use in the periphery contributing not only to haphazard developments but uneconomic utilisation of land.

PROPOSALS FOR LAND USE : 1984-2001

CDP Proposals

The CDP has proposed an area of 1,08,502 acres for development by 2001 (**Fig. 6.3**). Excluding the area of 50,100 acres already developed by 1983, the additional area proposed for development under different uses over a period of 17 years, comes to 50,402 acres. This has been worked out taking into account the requirements of the projected population of 7 million by 2001. Table 6.3 shows the area proposed for different uses by 2001. The maximum area (43,472 acres) is assigned for residential use, accounting for as much as 40 per cent of the conurbation area, followed by transportation which claims 22.3 per cent of the area and

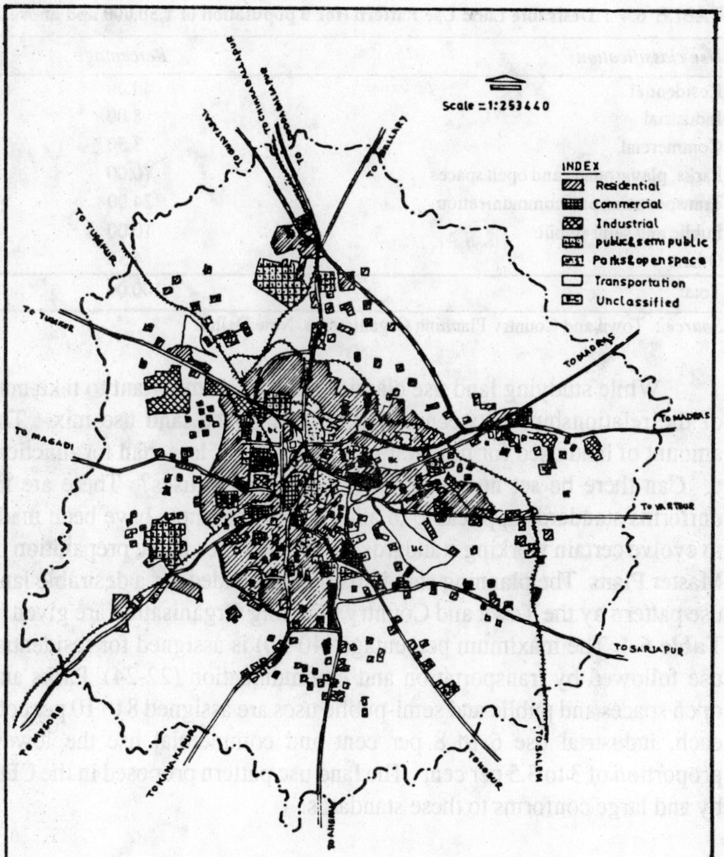

Fig. 6.1 : Bangalore : Existing Land use (1983)

Source : Comprehensive Development Plan Report of Bangalore 1984

parks and open spaces13.57%. The share of other uses, *viz.*, public and semi-public, industrial and commercial is 8.57 per cent, 6.8 per cent and 3.8 per cent respectively. An area of 5493 acres accounting for over 5 per cent occupied by Defence authorities is shown as unclassified.

TABLE 6.4 : **Desirable Land Use Pattern (for a population of 1,50,000 and above)**

Use classification	*Percentage*
Residential	40.00
Industrial	8.00
Commercial	3.50
Parks, playgrounds and open spaces	10.00
Transportation and communication	24.00
Public and semi-public	10.00
Others	4.50
Total	100.00

Source : Town and Country Planning Organisation, New Delhi.

While studying land use classification, it is important to take note of the relationships between different uses or the land use mix. The amount of land used for function *x* can be more or less than for function *y*. Can there be set norms or ratios for different uses? There are no uniforms standards applicable to all cities but attempts have been made to evolve certain working standards for Indian cities in the preparation of Master Plans. The planning standards recommended for a desirable land use pattern by the Town and Country Planning Organisation are given in **Table 6.4.** The maximum percentage (40-50) is assigned for residential use followed by transportation and communication (22-24). Parks and open spaces and public and semi-public uses are assigned 8 to 10 per cent each, industrial use 6 to 8 per cent and commercial use the lowest proportion of 3 to 3.5 per cent . The land use pattern proposed in the CDP by and large conforms to these standards.

Policy Implications

It is necessary to take note of the implications of the proposals in CDP in the context of Land Use Policy for Bangalore. A major policy objective enunciated in the CDP is curbing the growth of Bangalore Metropolitan Area and encouraging the other urban centres in the State. The rate of growth of population in the 'eighties and 'nineties is also assumed at a lower rate, *i.e.*, 5.5 per cent per annum compared to 7.6 per cent per annum during the seventies. The question is whether land use has been planned in a manner which would help achieve this objective.

It is important to note that the CDP provides for a very large planning area of 1,279 sq. km., about 250 per cent larger compared to that of ODP. Such a vast area is considered necessary "in view of the built up

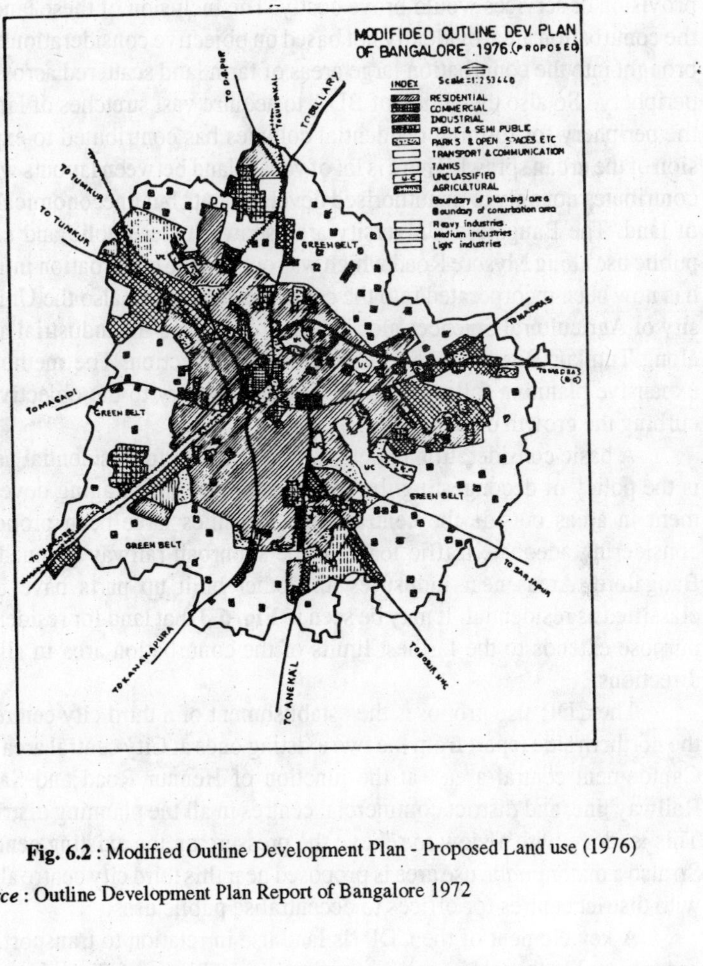

Fig. 6.2 : Modified Outline Development Plan - Proposed Land use (1976)

Source : Outline Development Plan Report of Bangalore 1972

area and conurbation area required up to the year 2001 and to provide an adequate green belt." There has, however, been no attempt to plan land use keeping in view the need to curb unrestricted physical expansion and to ensure optimum utilisation of land. An important factor that seems to have guided the planners in determining the areas for residential use is the compulsion to include lands proposed by the cooperative housing societies "included as per the decision taken during several meetings taken at government level and as decided by the BDA. . . . " (CDP, 1984). Most of these lands were agricultural and situated away from the city and where provision of services would prove costly. The inclusion of these lands in the conurbation area, evidently not based on objective considerations, has brought into the conurbation large areas of farm land scattered across the periphery. So also the policy of BDA to acquire vast stretches of land in the periphery for forming residential colonies has contributed to expansion of the urban sprawl. There is lot of vacant land between layouts which contributes not only to unauthorised developments but uneconomical use of land. The Bangalore University area shown under public and semi-public use along Mysore Road which was outside the conurbation in 1983 has now been incorporated into the conurbation area. So also the University of Agricultural Sciences along Bellary Road and the industrial areas along Tumkur Road and towards the eastern direction. The method of expansive planning followed by BDA runs contrary to the objective of curbing the growth of Bangalore.

A basic consideration in determining the area for residential needs is the policy of decongesting the central area and encouraging development in areas outside the central area. Densities have been proposed considering adequate traffic load for the suburban railway planned for Bangalore. Areas near industries and other built up parts have been classified as residential. It may be seen in **Fig. 6.3** that land for residential purpose extends to the farthest limits of the conurbation area in all the directions.

The CDP also proposes the establishment of a third city centre on the northern side (apart from the two existing ones at City central area and Cantonment central area), at the junction of Hennur Road and Salem Railway line, and district commercial centres in all the planning districts. This is done with a view to relieve the pressure on the existing centres. So also a major public use area is proposed near this third city centre along with district centres for offices to decentralise public uses.

A key element of the CDP is land use in relation to transport. In order to tackle the traffic and transportation problems of Bangalore city generated by the increase in population as well as number of vehicles, the plan has proposed strengthening the road network by a right road pattern and by introducing a rail transport system for the city. The land uses and population densities proposed in the plan are to a large extent based on the suggested railway alignments.

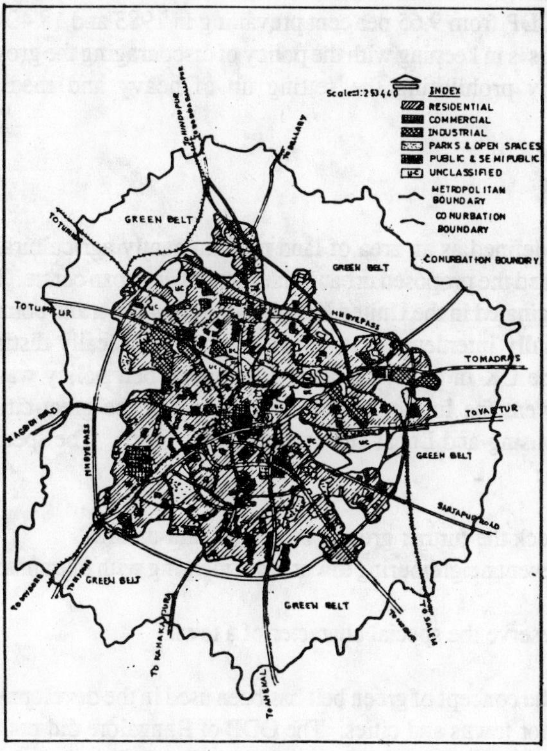

Fig. 6.3 : Comprehensive Development Plan - Proposed Land use (2001)

Source : Comprehensive Development Plan Report of Bangalore, 1984

Land Use Planning and Transportation Planning are closely related. Location, accessibility and commutation costs are important factors in determining the growth of a metropolitan city. In major western cities, location planning has been based mostly on mass transportation systems resulting in spatial expansion. Introducing a similar system in Indian cities gives rise to a number of problems. In the first place, it is highly capital intensive which our cities cannot afford. Secondly, it calls for synchronisation between Land Use and Transportation Planning which we are not able to achieve. These are mainly the reasons why the Railway Project for Bangalore has not taken shape even a decade after it was conceived.

The proportion of the area under industrial use has been reduced to 6.8 per cent in CDP from 9.65 per cent prevailing in 1983 and 18.40 per cent in ODP. This is in keeping with the policy of discouraging the growth of Bangalore by prohibiting the setting up of heavy and medium industries.

The Green Belt

A green belt is defined as an area of land predominantly agricultural in use, located around the proposed urbanisable limit of an urban centre. The concept as it originated in the United Kingdom was that town and country though functionally interdependent, should be kept physically distinct. Introduced in the UK in 1955, the aim of the green belt policy was in general "to prevent the further unrestricted sprawl of the great cities" (Ministry of Housing and Local Government, UK, 1955). The specific objectives were :

(a) to check the further growth of a large built up area;
(b) to prevent neighbouring towns from merging with one another; and
(c) to preserve the special character of a town.

In India, the concept of green belt has been used in the development plans prepared for towns and cities. The ODP of Bangalore did not use the term 'green belt' but referred to the 'Rural Tract'. It included 166 villages (95 villages fully and 71 partially) situated beyond the urban areas but within the Planning Area and covered an extent of 235 sq. km. The plan expressed its concern about preserving the rural features around the city. "Perhaps the most difficult problem in respect of this area is to preserve as many of its rural features as possible. While the regulations of building construction, if carefully carried out might secure this object to some extent, it is only by positive measures of agricultural development that it can be effectively ensured" (ODP, 1972). In fact, when the preparation of the CDP was taken up it was observed that heavy inroads were made into the green belt of ODP and a considerable extent of agricultural land was converted for urban uses.

The extent of loss of agricultural land over the years in the area surrounding Bangalore has been clearly brought out by a study undertaken by Indian Space Research Organisation. **Figures, 6.4** and **6.5** show that 69.3 per cent of the study area (652 sq. km.) was under agricultural use in 1912 whereas by 1985, this area declined to 32.6 per cent. During the same period the built up area increased from 6.1 to 48.7 per cent. A number of water bodies have also been lost yielding place to urban demands. *For example,* the Binnamangala tank has become a residential area and the Dharmambudi tank has become the Bangalore Bus Station.

A striking feature of the CDP is the provision of a wider green belt of nearly 840 sq. km. accounting for 65 per cent of the total planning area. This has been justified on the ground that in the past the green belt was getting shifted on account of encroachments. A pattern has therefore been evolved according to which the green belt protrudes into the built up area in the form of wedges as shown in **Fig. 6.3.** In fact, a considerable part of the earlier green belt of ODP seen in **Fig. 6.2** has been earmarked for development in CDP. The difficulties in preserving the green belt, however, continue amidst pressures for conversion of land for non-green purposes. Co-operative housing societies have in particular drawn heavily on the green belt area to establish residential colonies. The huge area earmarked for green belt in the CDP has added to the problems in implementation, especially as much of this area is owned by private persons.

The green belt policy of Bangalore needs to be reviewed, and a new approach adopted. In the first place, the purpose of green belt must be clearly defined and issues like its size, pattern and the regulations governing its use must be gone into.

The problems of green belt are not peculiar to Bangalore or to India. An assessment of the green belts in Britain has led to the conclusion that "while they have caused more problems than they have solved, they should be directed more specifically to the project in particular and to more carefully defined facets of landscape" (David Thomas, 1976). Hence, the emphasis today is more on open spaces and not necessarily on a continuous stretch of green belt. Open space should :

(1) give structure, shape and form separating clusters, preserving wedges, and giving identity to urban communities and yet unite them through parks and playgrounds, and
(2) draw a 'limit of development line' both within the city and around the city to prevent sporadic sprawl.

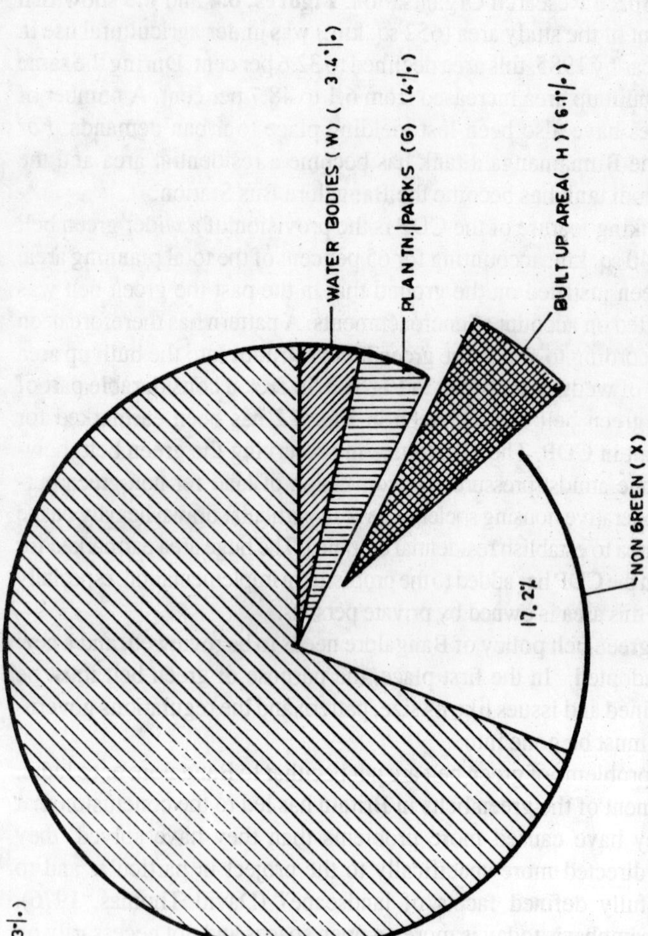

SOURCE - Indian Space Research Organisation

BASED ON DETAILS DERIVED FROM SURVEY OF INDIA MAP . 1912-26

Fig. 6.4: Land Use of Bangalore and Surrounding (1912)

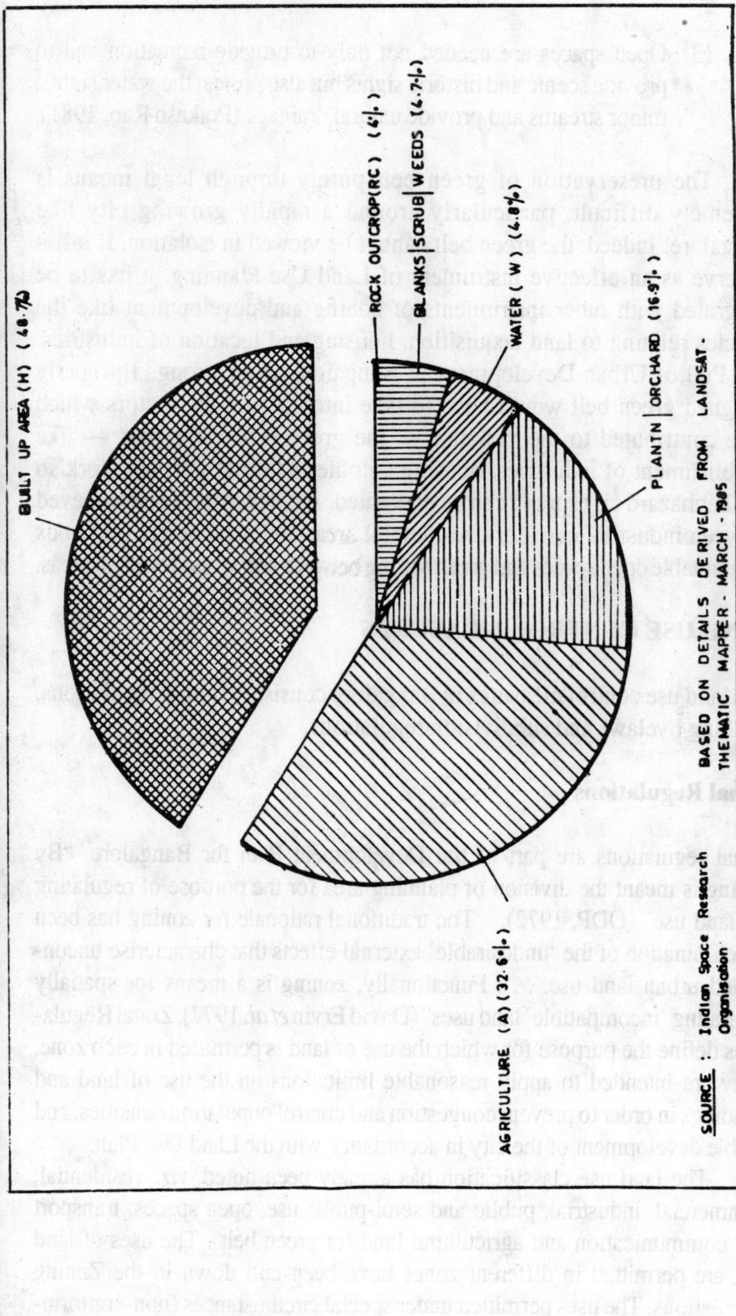

Fig. 6.5 : Land Use of Bangalore and Surrounding (1985)

(3) Open spaces are needed not only to provide recreation and to provide scenic and historic sights but also protect the water sights, minor streams and provide natural drainage (Prakash Rao, 1981).

The preservation of green belt purely through legal means is extremely difficult, particularly around a rapidly growing city like Bangalore. Indeed, the green belt cannot be viewed in isolation. If it has to serve as an effective instrument of Land Use Planning, it has to be integrated with other instruments of zoning and development like the policies relating to land acquisition, housing and location of industries. The Pull of Urban Development in Bangalore being strong, a properly designed green belt would have to take into account the factors which have contributed to the violation of the green belt in the past — like establishment of industries, housing colonies and transport net work so that haphazard city sprawl can be prevented. A balance has to be achieved between industrial corridors, residential areas and rural neighbourhoods with suitable open spaces and green setting between and around built up areas.

LAND USE CONTROL MEASURES

The land use control measures in Bangalore consists of zonal regulations, building byelaws and subdivision regulations.

Zonal Regulations

Zonal regulations are part of the Development Plan for Bangalore. "By zoning is meant the division of planning area for the purpose of regulating the land use" (ODP, 1972). "The traditional rationale for zoning has been the elimination of the 'undesirable' external effects that characterise uncontrolled urban land use. . . . Functionally, zoning is a means for spatially separating 'incompatible' land uses" (David Ervin *et al.* 1977). Zonal Regulations define the purpose for which the use of land is permitted in each zone. They are intended to apply reasonable limitations on the use of land and buildings in order to prevent congestion and control population densities, and enable development of the city in accordance with the Land Use Plan.

The land use classification has already been noted, *viz.*, residential, commercial, industrial, public and semi-public use, open spaces, transport and communication and agricultural land (or green belt). The uses of land that are permitted in different zones have been laid down in the Zoning Regulations. The uses permitted under special circumstances (non-conforming use) have also been specified for different zones. *For example,* in the residential zone, uses that are normally permitted are dwellings, places of public worship, schools offering general educational courses, libraries etc. The other uses that are permitted under special circumstances in the residential zones include government offices, public utility buildings, hospitals, huller flour mills. In the retail business zone, uses that are normally permitted are offices, shops, service establishments like hospitals, laundry, barber shops, schools, certain service industries, etc. Uses that are permitted under special circumstances include automobile workshops and manufacturing establishments employing not more than ten labourers.

Building Byelaws

The Building Byelaws which form part of the zoning regulations prescribe the set-backs, maximum plot coverage and Floor Area Ratio (FAR) for different areas. Based on these regulations, the Bangalore City Corporation has framed separate Building Byelaws which came into force from 31st October, 1984 and are followed by the Corporation and the BDA to regulate construction activity.

The city has been divided into the following three areas for the purpose of regulating the construction of buildings:

A. Intensely populated areas;
B. Central Administration Area and its surroundings;
C. All areas other than the areas comprised in A & B.

The above areas have been demarcated in the map and annexed to the byelaws **(Fig. 6.6)**.

The maximum plot coverage,[1] FAR[2] and the height permitted for different areas are given in **Table 6.5.**

TABLE 6.5 : **Building Byelaws —Basic parameters**

Zone	*Maximum Plot Coverage (%age)*	*Floor Area Ratio*	*Maximum hieght (Metres)*
Residential Buildings			
A	75	0.75-1.25	14
B	65-45	1 -1.50	11-17
C	60-40	1.25-1.75	11-17
Commercial Buildings			
A	80-60	1 -1.50	7-17
B	70-50	1.25-1.75	11-17
C	65-45	1.50-2.00	11-27

Source : Building Byelaws, Bangalore City Corporation.

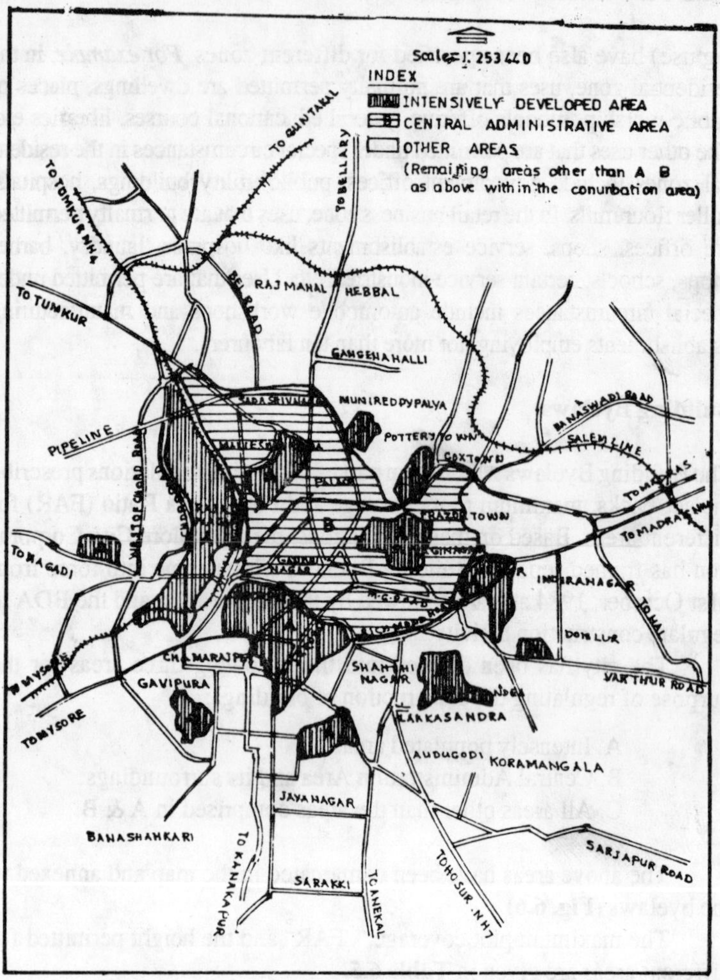

Fig. 6.6 : Classification of Bangalore unde Building Byelaws

Source : Comphrensive Development Plan Report of Bengalore, 1984

High rise buildings[3] with higher FAR have been permitted only for commercial purposes on eight roads in the city - Dickenson Road, Brigade Road, Geetanjali Talkies Road, Wheeler Road, East of Chord Road, MG Road and Residency Road. The FAR allowed for high rise buildings on these roads ranges from 2.5 to 3.5 and a maximum of ground +13 floors is permitted. Group housing may be permitted in the areas specially designed for the purpose by BDA.

The number of building licenses sanctioned in Bangalore by the Bangalore City Corporation from 1970-71 shows that building activity has not registered a steady growth (**Table 6.6**). On the other hand, it has shown variations from time to time. The highest number of licenses was issued in the year 1979-80 (8,632) and the lowest number (4,998) in 1986-87. In fact, after reaching the level of 6,440 in 1984-85, there was a decline to 5,520 in 1985-86 and 4,998 in 1986-87.

TABLE 6.6 : **Building licences sanctioned by Bangalore City Corporation**

Year	*No. of licences Sanctioned*
1970-71	7,999
1971-72	6,922
1972-73	7,466
1973-74	6.971
1974-75	7,962
1975-76	7,529
1976-77	5,702
1977-78	8,386
1978-79	5,934
1979-80	8,632
1980-81	7,350
1981-82	7,428
1982-83	6,987
1983-84	6,628
1984-85	8,440
1985-86	5,520
1986-87	4,998
1987-88	5,109

Source : Bangalore City Corporation Records.

Vertical versus Horizontal Development : The development in Bangalore city has traditionally been more extensive rather than intensive. Two factors have contributed to such a phenomenon :

(a) there are scope for expansion on all the sides of the city, and

(b) the zoning regulations have not favoured vertical development (except for commercial developments on certain roads as per the Byelaws of 1984, as already noted).

The growth in population and the economic activity accompanied by the rising demand for land during the last two decades has, however, altered the conception about mere horizontal expansion.

Construction of high rise building in Bangalore has shown a fluctuating trend. **Table 6.7** shows the number of licences sanctioned for high rise buildings from 1981-82 to 1987-88. Totally, 186 high rise buildings were permitted to be constructed during this seven year period. After reaching a high of 52 buildings in 1984-85, the number declined in subsequent years coming down to as low as 12 in 1987-88. An important reason for the declining trend noticed after 1984-85 seems to be the introduction of the new building Byelaws which came into force from 31st October 1984 which imposed stricter standards compared to the regulations that were followed earlier. It is relevant to point out here that buildings with ground +3 floors appear to be popular in Bangalore. During the same period of seven years from 1981-82, as many as 238 such buildings were sanctioned (**Table 6.7**). One reason could be that ground +3 floors is not treated as a high-rise building and the builder is subject to fewer controls. Secondly, the byelaws do not permit more than ground +4 floors for residential buildings.

TABLE 6.7 : **High Rise Building Licences sanctioned by Bangalore City Corporation**

Year	*G+4*	*G+5*	*G+6*	*G+7*	*G+8*	*G+9*	*G+10*	*G+13*	*Total*	*G+*
1981-82	6	2	4	4	1	1	—	—	18	30
1982-83	2	2	3	—	—	—	1	—	8	32
1983-84	40	—	3	2	—	—	—	—	45	34
1984-85	49	—	3	—	—	—	—	—	52	15
1985-86	13	3	2	2	—	—	—	2	22	44
1986-87	20	3	2	2	—	—	—	2	29	42
1987-88	9	2	1	—	—	—	—	—	12	41
Total	139	12	18	10	1	1	1	4	186	238

Note : G Ground Floor.
Source : Bangalore City Corporation Records.

The building byelaws have attracted the following comments :

(a) the procedure for obtaining building licence is cumbersome, particularly for a high-rise building where clearances are to be obtained from a number of authorities;

(b) intensive development is not possible except in a few areas in respect of commercial buildings;

(c) the provision for offstreet parking is inadequate resulting in parking problems; and

(d) standards prescribed are rigid with hardly any scope for relaxation.

Subdivision Regulations

Sanction for the subdivision of a plot is to be obtained from the BDA under Section 17 of the Karnataka Town and Country Planning Act. The following requirements are to be satisfied before a plot is subdivided. The minimum size of the plot should be as given below :

Agricultural Zone	—	0.4 hectares
Residential Zone	—	90 sq. metres
Rural Gramatana other Zone	—	56 sq. metres

The minimum width of streets and lanes in residential areas have been laid down. For instance, in respect of minor roads the width has to be 18 metres, for a major road 24.50 metres and for an arterial road 33 metres. Separate building lines have been prescribed for important roads in Bangalore. In practice, it is observed that subdivision regulations are not strictly followed. There are violations of the building line on many roads. In private layouts, narrow roads have been framed with less than prescribed widths. These are found to have an adverse effect on further development, especially where road widening is called for.

Deviations from Zonal Planning

A Development Plan is normally supposed to hold good at least for a period of fifteen years. In practice, however, it is observed that there are a number of deviations from the zonal land use plan even within a five year period. The encroachment into the green belt and consequent conversion of agricultural land has already been dealt with. Even after the CDP came into force, conversions have been taking place on a pretty large scale. During a brief period of two years—1986-88, permission has been given by the Deputy Commissioner, Bangalore District for conversion of agricultural land as noted below :

(a) Bangalore North Taluk	47 acres
(b) Bangalore South Taluk	53 acres
(c) Anekal Taluk	69 acres

The majority of conversions are for residential purposes and some for industrial/commercial purposes.

It is possible for a person to change the use of land by obtaining necessary permission from the competent authority. According to Section 14 of the Karnataka Town and Country Planning Act, every land use, every change in land use and every development shall conform to the development plan. Any change in land use or development can be made only after obtaining the written permission from the Planning Authority. The number of cases where permission has been given by the BDA for exchange of land use is shown in Table 6.8. 301 changes have been permitted in a period of seven years from 1981-87. During the three years following the coming into force of the CDP (1985-87), as many as 197 changes have been permitted, 126 of them in a single year in 1987. The maximum demand is for commercial use of land. The pattern of change of land use over the years reveals that at the core of the city and at the intermediate level, the tendency is towards commercial uses whereas at the periphery the pull is for residential purposes.

TABLE 6.8 : **Change of land use permitted — 1981 to 1987**

Year	*For Commercial (no.)*	*For Residential (no.)*	*For Industrial (no.)*	*Total (no.)*
1981	6	—	—	6
1982	34	2	1	37
1983	9	2	1	12
1984	49	—	—	49
1985	20	1	3	24
1986	40	5	2	47
1987	106	17	3	126
Total	264	27	10	301

Source : Bangalore Development Authority Records.

Apart from the sanctioned deviations from the plan, the fact of unauthorised changes must also be taken note of. No accurate figures are available about such unauthorised conversions. But it is noticed that even in recently developed extensions, a number of residential areas are gradually turning commercial. Residences are being converted to educational institutions, nursing homes, office premises and retail shops. The following are some examples of deviation from the land use plan :

(a) along the Hosur Road (near Wilson Garden and Lakkasandra), commercial shops have come up in the area meant for residential use;

(b) commercial activities have come up on either side of the 30th Cross Road in Jayanagar, although the area is earmarked for residential use;

(c) a number of industries and a polytechnic have come up in green belt area after Krishnarajapura;

(d) along the Bellary Road, industrial development is noticed in some parts of the area shown as agricultural university;

(e) area's earmarked for residential purposes along the I and II Main Road of Gandhinagar, are being used for commercial activities; and

(f) residential buildings including apartments have come up in the area earmarked for the purpose of park near the Sanatorium.

In the matter of conversion of agricultural land for non-agricultural purposes, there is a legal ambiguity. While the Deputy Commissioner is permitted to grant such conversion under the Land Revenue Act, the permission of the Planning Authority is necessary where the land comes under the Planning area. In practice, the Deputy Commissioner has been granting permission for conversions without reference to the Planning Authority. This has resulted in mushroom growth of residential pockets around Bangalore. Even lands which come under the Green Belt according to the Development Plan are being converted for non-agricultural uses resulting in built-up developments. The State Government, therefore, brought about an amendment to the Karnataka Land Revenue Act in 1984 to the effect that no permission shall be granted for using agricultural land lying within the limits of the green belt, for any purpose, when a certain area is declared as 'Green Belt'. The matter went up to the High Court of Karnataka which ruled that "change of use of land lying within the planning area can be effected only with the permission obtained from the planning authority and action of the permission secured from the Deputy Commissioner would no longer be lawful and the Planning Authority is empowered to prevent any person acting on the basis of the permission granted by the Deputy Commissioner under Section 95 of the Land Revenue Act."[1] In other words, any change of land use with the permission of the Planning Authority alone is considered lawful. However, the issue is still not finally settled and the Deputy Commissioner continues to give permission for conversion of agricultural land.

The zoning regulations, as already noted, clearly specify the uses permitted in each zone and the non-conforming uses permissible under special circumstances. Thus the scope for discretion in the grant of

permission for change of land use is almost eliminated. Nevertheless, the law has vested the power of granting such permissions in the Planning Authority. The circumstances under which such change in land use can be permitted have, however, not been laid down anywhere in the law. No guidelines have been formulated by the Planning Authority or the Government in this regard. The result is, in practice, the BDA exercises full discretionary power, although the prior approval of Government has to be obtained before the commencement certificate containing the permission for change in land use is actually issued to the applicant.

INDUSTRIAL LOCATION POLICY

Industrialisation is part of the process of urbanisation. In the context of Urban Planning and Urban Land Use Policy, industrial development has to be considered from two angles—location in a city area and industrial dispersal.

Intra-city Location

The location of industries in a growing city influences its urban pattern. As per the models of industrial location (described in Chapter 2), industries may be located in different areas of the city depending on the nature of the particular industry — market oriented industries in central areas, manufacturing industries in suburbs and integrated industries along communication lines. In practice, however, locations do not follow such clear demarcations. Factors like availability of land, the price of land and infrastructural facilities influence locations.

Bangalore is a highly industrialised area. It houses a large number of industries in the public and private sectors. The industries in Bangalore have been located in different parts of the city and in different directions. The bigger industries have been established mostly on the eastern side (HAL-BEML, area and NGEF-ITI area) and the northwestern side (HMT-BEL area). Industrial estates have sprung up in Rajajinagar (western side) and along the highways on Tumkur Road and Hosur Road. Small scale and medium industries have come up along all the highway roads — Tumkur Road, Madras Road, Hosur Road and Kanakapura Road.

Initially, no specific policy seems to have guided the location and development of industries in and around Bangalore. The easy and cheap availability of land around the city in the 'forties and 'fifties facilitated location of industries virtually in any direction. Another vital considera-

tion was the transport and communication network. It was quite convenient to set up the units along or in the vicinity of the highways. Other important factors which contributed to the early industrialisation of the city were the availability of water and power at cheap rates, the relatively peaceful industrial relations prevailing in the State and the favourable climate of the city. The overall impact of industrialisation has been a rapid growth in population, generation of economic activity and a heavy strain on the civic services and infrastructure of the city. The pattern of industrial location has contributed to the city's sprawl and ribbon development. The area occupied by industries went up from 8.3 to 9.65 per cent of the developed area of the city.

Dispersal Policy

The industrialisation of Bangalore and the relative backwardness and underdevelopment of several other parts of the State prompted the State Government to formulate a policy for reducing the disparity in the degree of development between different regions of the State and to bring about balanced development. To begin with, government was committed to a policy of rapid industrialisation in the entire State. A number of decisions were taken from time to time extending several concessions and incentives to entrepreneurs to start new industries in and around Bangalore. Hence, in November 1971, Government thought that "with a view to avoid further concentration of industries in and around Bangalore, it has become necessary to disperse them to industrially backward areas by offering additional incentives, wherever, necessary" (Government of Karnataka, 1971). Eleven districts were identified as industrially backward for the purpose of extending this concession.

In 1980, the Government of India issued an industrial policy statement containing government's locational policy to correct regional imbalances in industrialisation and to ensure environmental protection. According to this policy, "setting up of new industries or extension of existing industries will be discouraged within urban area limits of metropolitan cities with a population of more than ten lakhs." Concessions like exemption from licensing in certain cases, the scheme of delicensing in respect of certain units and the benefit of re-endorsement were not made applicable to industrial undertakings located in metropolitan cities. In an important policy decision in October 1972, the State Government divided the State into four zones with a view to ensure dispersal of industries. Zone-I (classified as industrially more developed area) covered Bangalore

Urban Agglomeration, Bangalore South and North taluks and Mysore City Corporation area. The package of incentives and concessions were made available in different degrees to the areas covered in Zones-II, III and IV. Zone I was not eligible for any of these incentives and concessions.

In spite of the policy of discouragement of fresh industrialisation in Bangalore, the capital city continues to be the most attractive place in the State for entrepreneurs. Although no major large scale industry comparable to the giant units like HAL, HMT might have come up in the recent past, the growth of small and medium scale industries continues unabated. From a mere 925 units registered in 1970-71, the number had grown to over 18,000 in 1987-88, *i.e.,* about 20 times. The reasons for such development are the following :

(a) The policy of discouraging setting up of new industries in Bangalore also contained relaxations. *For example,* although investment subsidy was not permissible in Zone-I, interest subsidy on term loans was extended. Similarly price preference for small scale units for the first-five years was also available. Again in just about one year after the commencement of the policy, modifications were effected excluding two industrial areas — Veerasandra and Bommasandra in Bangalore Urban Agglomeration from Zone-I. The Electronic City of Bangalore was shifted from Zone-I to Zone-II.

(b) Two Government Organisations, *viz.,* the Karnataka Industrial Areas Development Board and the Karnataka State Small Industries Development Corporation contributed to the promotion of industrial development in and around Bangalore — the former in respect of medium and large scale industries and the latter in respect of small scale industries. The largest number of Industrial Areas (ten) were set up in Bangalore district by the KIADB and the largest number of industrial estates (sixteen) set up by KSSIDC also happened to be in Bangalore. An analysis of the infrastructural facilities created — like posts and telegraphs offices, banks, telephone exchange, electrical substation, etc., reveals that the industrial areas and estates in Bangalore district are better serviced than those in other parts of the State.

(c) Bangalore enjoys certain advantages like an airport, facilitating easy and quick access to and from other major cities in the

country, good educational and medical facilities and other conveniences of an administrative centre of a capital city—all of which act as sort of natural incentives for setting up industries. Lack of certian concessions extended in other backward areas which suffer from locational disadvantage has not acted as a dempener to industrial investment in Bangalore.

All these developments under core the need for proper coordination between Industrial Development and Urban Development Policies for formulating a rational location policy.

NEW APPROACHES TO PLANNING

The Master Plan approach emphasises physical planning which is essentially concerned with specification of the use to which land should be put, and control over physical development. The CDP of Bangalore does little more than this, although it contains certain proposals for development of housing and other socio-economic facilities. These proposals are based mainly on land requirements for projected populations. It is necessary to move away from this traditional concept of planning and adopt a new approach to deal with the emerging needs of city development. The following suggestions are made.

(a) In the first place, land use planning must be considered as part of the general planning process. The role of a city as a generator of economic growth must be recognised and any planning exercise must concern itself with the major functions a city performs. Land Use Planning must be related to these city functions. Employment, for instance, is one such major function. Location of economic activities must be based on considerations in regard to transport alignments, communication facilities, environment and the socio-economic profile of the people living in the city. All this calls for integration of spatial planning and economic planning.

(b) Secondly, land use planning must aim at proper utilisation of land. The haphazard growth of Bangalore on the fringes, the ribbon extensions and vacant lands in developed areas indicate inefficient and uneconomic use of land. "The existing Town Planning practices are largely aimed at controlling land use patterns rather than optimising land use in terms of economic returns, employment generation, provision of shelter and the raising of additional resources for city development" (NCU, 1988). Hence planning for land as a resource must replace planning of land as an exercise in zoning. Identification of vacant land and areas of uneconomical use in the city is a first step in this direction.

(c) Land use or development control measures now in practice are oriented more towards regulation than development. "The classes of permitted development are stated in terms of the nature of the use than of its impact on the environment." (Mcloughlin, 1973). The rigid prescriptions for land use and building purposes do not match the planning problems facing the authorities. Low densities, for instance, reduce the scope for optimum utilisation of space. While controls are necessary, they must help and not hinder the process of urban development. They must be rationalised so as to promote development activity, especially low cost housing in the context of the serious shortage of housing in Bangalore as in many other cities. An innovative measure that can be introduced is the 'planned unit development zoning' where by clustering uses and consolidating open spaces, substantial land can be saved.

(d) Industrial development has, by and large, taken place without any relationship to the urban planning process. Future policies for development have to be formulated in a regional and statewise perspective. The State Government has identified certain growth centres[5] for accelerated industrial development. Necessary infrastructure has to be provided in these centres to attract fresh investments. Similarly, transport and communication must be strengthened to facilitate faster movement of traffic. Provision of broad gauge railway line between Bangalore and Mysore and between Bangalore and Hubli-Belgaum and a new railway line between Hubli and Karwar, regular air service to Mysore and Hubli will act as incentives for location of industries in urban centres other than Bangalore. Location policy should aim at achieving balanced urbanisation of the State.

In the metropolitan area of Bangalore, public policy must aim at promoting hitch industries which are non-polluting, and other economic activities which do not require much physical space and are less labour intensive. This will be in keeping with the policy of curbing large scale industrial development in the city and at the same time it will contribute to the economic growth of the metropolis.

NOTES

1. The maximum area of the plot or site that can be covered with building. (Writ Appeal No. 1938/39/80, 1987)
2. FAR or Floor Area Ratio is the quotient obtained by dividing the total covered area on all floors by the area of the plot.
3. A highrise building is a building with more than for floors *i.e.* ground floor + three floors and above requiring the provision of a lift.
4. Group housing means a group of multistoreyed housing for more than one dwelling unit where land is owned jointly (as in the case of co-operative societies or the public agencies such as local authorities, housing boards, etc.) and the construction is undertaken by one Agency/Authority.
5. Dharwad, Hassan and Raichur.

7

LAND ACQUISITION AND DISPOSAL

One of the basic objectives of Urban Land Policy is to supply land for specific purposes and to meet the needs of urban development. The means employed to achieve this objective is acquisition of land and redistributing or allocating the same for the purpose for which it is acquired. Thus land acquisition helps to achieve the other policy objectives like widening the base of land ownership, providing the poor access to land, efficient allocation of urban land and encouraging cooperative and individual effort in land development and house building.

Public Land Acquisition Policies and Procedures have developed in response to the land requirements of Public Housing Projects, the Development of a Sound Infrastructure and Public Utility Projects (Darin-Drabkin, 1977). In Bangalore, the policy of land acquisition followed by the planners bears a close relationship to the evolution of Urban Land Use Policy for the City. The long tradition of planned development in Bangalore enabled acquisition and allocation of land for specific uses—primarily residential and industrial. The Bangalore City Improvement Trust Board (1945) went in for large scale acquisition for formation of residential extensions and also for an industrial suburb in Rajajinagar. For this purpose its jurisdiction was extended to a number of villages beyond the Corporation limits. The BDA, its successor organisation continued the process of acquiring land mainly to meet the housing needs of the people. The growth of the city also necessitated provision of space for infrastructure like roads and drainage, accommodation for slum dwellers and other development activities. The development plans of Bangalore (ODP & CDP) envisaged additional requirements of land for various purposes, as already noted in Chapter 6. Much of the land to be developed and allocated as per the Land Use Plan had to come from land acquisition. The Land Acquisition Policy for Bangalore has (though not expressly stated) mainly aimed at providing land for the following purposes :

(i) Housing for individuals and organisations;
(ii) Infrastructure to meet the requirements of transport, traffic, water supply, drainage etc.; and
(iii) Industrial development;

The process of land acquisition and disposal in Bangalore is discussed under the following heads :

(i) Legal Elements and Methods of Acquisition;
(ii) Problems of Implementation;
(iii) Land Acquisition by Cooperative House Building Societies;
(iv) Land Acquisition under the Urban Land Ceiling Act.
(v) Land Disposal Policy; and
(vi) New Approaches to Acquisition and Disposal.

LEGAL ELEMENTS AND METHODS OF ACQUISITION

Land can be acquired in Bangalore under the following laws :

1. The Land Acquisition (Karnataka Extension and Amendment) Act, 1961.
2. The Karnataka Industrial Areas Development Board Act, 1966.
3. The Karnataka Slum Improvement and Clearance Act, 1973.
4. The Bangalore Development Authority Act, 1976,
5. The Urban Land Ceiling and Regulation Act, 1976.

The above laws provide for different methods of acquisition. They are as follows :

1. Compulsory acquisition under the Land Acquisition Act and the Slum Improvement and Clearance Act.
2. Acquisition through negotiation under the Acts at (4) and (5) above.
3. Acquisition of surplus land under the Urban Land Ceiling Act.

Compulsory Acquisition

The legislation most commonly resorted to, *viz.*, the Land Acquisition Act lays down the following five major steps for compulsory acquisition of private land :

1. Issue of a preliminary notification under Section 4(1) of the Act notifying the purpose for which the land is needed, and inviting objections.
2. Filing objections within 30 days and hearing of objections within a period of six weeks from the last date of filing of objections,
3. Issue of declaration by Government that the particulars land is needed for a public purpose under Section 6 of the Act.
4. Issue of public notice inviting claims for compensation from the interested persons. After enquiry, passing of award determining the area of the land to be acquired, the compensation to be paid and the apportionment of compensation among the interested persons.
5. Taking possession of the land and notifying in the official gazette. The land acquired shall then vest in the government free from all encumbrances.

Under the Karnataka Slum Improvement and Clearance Act, land can be acquired for the purpose of executing any work of improvement in a slum area or for redeveloping the area or for rehabilitating the slum dwellers. The land to be acquired will have to be within, adjoining or surrounded by slum area. The procedure for acquisition under this Act is very simple compared to the procedure to be followed under the Land Acquisition Act, 1894. All that the law requires is to give a notice to the owner or interested person in the land to show cause why the land should be acquired and after considering the representations, if any, Government may pass orders for acquisition by issuing a notifications in the Gazette. Thereafter the land will vest absolutely in government free from all encumbrances.

Another vital difference between this Act and the Land Acquisition Act is in respect of payment of compensation. What is payable in respect of land acquired under the Slum (Improvement and Clearance) Act is only an amount which shall be one hundred times the property tax payable in respect of such land on the date of publication of notice under Section 17 and not the market rate as required under the Land Acquisition Act.

Acquisition Through Negotiation

The Bangalore Development Authority Act and the Karnataka Industrial Area Development Board Act provide for acquisition of land for executing their development schemes by agreement with land owners for the purchase of such land. The compensation to be paid can be determined by agreement with the owner after negotiations.

Acquisition of Surplus Land

Under the Urban Land Ceiling Act, no person can hold vacant land in Bangalore Urban Agglomeration in excess of 1,000 sq.m. Land in excess of this ceiling limit is to be compulsorily acquired. The following procedure is followed in acquiring such land.

Every person holding vacant land in excess of the ceiling limit has to file a statement before the competent authority containing details of all the vacant lands held by him. The Competent Authority will conduct necessary enquiry and determine the vacant land held by the person concerned in excess of the ceiling limit. Thereafter, a notification shall be published in the Gazette declaring the excess vacant land to be deemed to have been acquired by the State Government.

The person whose excess vacant land has been acquired is paid an amount which can be considered a nominal compensation. The amount will be equal to 8⅓ times the net average annual income actually derived from such land for the five consecutive years preceding the date of publication of the notification issued under Section 10(1) of the Act. In case where no income is derived from such vacant land, the amount to be paid shall be calculated at a rate not exceeding Rs. 10 per sq.mtr. in the case of vacant land in Category 'A' and 'B' and Rs. 5 per sq.meter in Category 'C' and 'D'. The mode of payment is—25 per cent of the amount or Rs. 25,000 whichever is less will be paid in cash and the balance in negotiable bonds redeemable after 20 years carrying an interest of 5 per cent per annum.

Under Section 20 of the Act, the State Government is empowered to grant exemption to persons on two grounds :

(a) in the public interest, or
(b) if the application of the provisions of the Act would cause undue hardship for such persons.

Where such exemption is granted, the surplus land of persons concerned will not be acquired

PROBLEMS IN IMPLEMENTATION

Land acquisition is beset with numerous problems. They pertain mainly to the following aspects :

(a) Procedural and administrative delays;
(b) Valuation of property and determination of compensation;
(c) Litigation.

(a) Procedural Delays

The procedure prescribed for acquisition by law itself is quite elaborate. This is to be justified on the ground that acquisition involves the private rights of individuals and a person and his family are deprived of the property they hold, which may often happen to be the only source of their livelihood. Secondly, land must be acquired only when it is absolutely necessary and it is, therefore, essential to examine in detail the need for acquisition, after giving sufficient opportunity to the persons interested to put forward their case. Thirdly, as huge amounts are paid by way of compensation, it must be ensured that public money is spent in a useful manner in public interest and not wasted in unnecessary ventures. The State Government summed up the 'care' to be exercised in these matters while issuing instructions to the Land Acquisition Officers thus :

> "The Land Acquisition Officers should be careful in handling public funds. They should see that well-reasoned awards which should be fair to all parties, based on full and proper data are drafted. They should follow strictly and scrupulously the norms laid down in the Land Acquisition Act and the rules framed thereunder. The award-approving authorities should see that the land acquisition officers pass the awards on the basis of such full data after proper verification and personal satisfaction about the reasonableness of the same" (Government of Karnataka, 1980).

While the intention of the Legislature in prescribing an elaborate procedure can be appreciated, in practice it results in inordinate delay.

Data collected on the actual time taken to complete acquisition proceedings reveal that the average time taken by BDA, the premier land acquisition and development agency in Bangalore Metropolitan Area, is four to five years. In some cases it has taken as long as ten years. Particulars in respect of ten cases furnished in **Table 7.1** would show that delay occurs at both stages—between issue of preliminary and final notification, and taking possession. The gap between taking possession of the first bit and the last bit of land in the same project extends to 6-7 years. Such delays are common to other acquiring authorities like the City Corporation and the Revenue Department. In the case of Karnataka Industrial Area Development Board, however, the acquisition has been speedier (possession has been taken just two months after issue of preliminary notification in some cases), wherever, land has been acquired through negotiations.

The factors contributing to delay are mainly two-fold. Administrative, and litigation. The administrative reasons are the following :

(i) changes are made in the site selected for a project after acquisition proceedings have been initiated. This involves withdrawal of such proceedings and issue of fresh notification;
(ii) enquiry proceedings both at the stage of Section 5-A and before passing of the award get prolonged;
(iii) delay in the publication of notifications in the gazette;
(iv) delay in taking possession of the land after the award is passed.

(b) Litigation

The most fruitful source of delay in most acquisition cases is litigation. The interested parties approach the courts of law and obtain stay orders at different stages in the acquisition proceedings. In such circumstances, the Land Acquisition Officer has to wait till disposal of the cases in the court before he can proceed further. The number of cases pertaining to Bangalore Development Authority pending in courts for different periods is shown in Table 7.2. There are 270 cases pending in respect of five schemes. All of them are pending for a period extending from over one year to over seven years. Persons approach the court for different reasons —questioning the purpose of acquisition, on procedural and technical matters and disputing the amount of compensation. The last mentioned reason, however, need not stand in the way of going through acquisition proceedings and taking possession of land.

TABLE 7.1 : **Land Acquisitiopn by Bangalore Development Authority**

Scheme	*Area notified (acres)*	*Area acquired (acres)*	*Date of preliminary notification*	*Date of final notification*	*Year of taking possession of land*
Hennur Road Banasavadi Road Layout	1,771	923	21.3.77	12.6.80	between 1982 and 1988
Rajamahal Vilas II Stage	1,334	1,140	24.2.77	2.8.78	between 1981 and 1988
Nandini Layout	786	885	16.1.77	1.1.79	between 1981 and 1986
Hennur Road Bellary Road I Stage	875	550	27.6.78	24.3.85	between 1986 and 1988
Hennur Road Bellary Road II Stage	1,137	200	21.9.78	6.6.85	between 1987 and 1988
East of NGEF	523	166	28.5.84	23.10.86	between 1987 and 1988
Hosur Road — Sarjapur Road	1,664	850	15.12.84	13.11.86	between 1987 and 1988
Chandra Layout	621	335	10.7.77	19.5.78	between 1970 and 1982
Nagarabhavi Layout	520	204	12.8.82	16.8.85	between 1986 and 1988
BTM Scheme	1,703	969	19.9.77	7.7.78	between 1980 and 1986

TABLE 7.2 : **Land Acquisition cases of Bangalore Development Authority pending in Courts in 1988**

Scheme	*No. of cases pending*	*1-2 years*	*2-3 years*	*3-4 years*	*4-5 years*	*5-6 years*	*6-7 years*	*over seven years*
Hennur Road Banasavadi Road	57	—	3	17	23	14	—	—
Hennur-Bellary I stage	70	—	—	14	17	22	8	9
Hennur-Bellary II stage	58	—	—	44	—	—	14	—
Further Extension of Mahalakshmi Layout (Nandini)	63	—	—	—	30	10	—	23
East of NGEF	22	13	8	—	—	1	—	—
Total	270	13	11	75	70	47	22	32

(c) Valuation of Property

The basic consideration in the valuation of the property according to the Land Acquisition Act is the market value. However, valuation has continued to be a ticklish problem. In view of the difficulties faced by Land Acquisition Officers in the matter of valuation, the State Government has issued guidelines from time to time on the manner of determining compensation. According to the guidelines issued in 1963, the following procedure is to be followed :

(a) in determining the compensation, the sub-registry statistics pertaining to the sales of similar properties in the vicinity of the properties to be acquired as on the date of preliminary notification must be taken into consideration;
(b) in the case of agricultural lands, the value of individual lands should be determined after taking into consideration the distance from main road, the distance from the village proper, the availability of water facilities etc.
(c) in the case of non-agricultural lands, land actually put to non-agricultural uses, *i.e.*, construction of buildings should be treated as building sites and valued accordingly;
(d) the value of lands can also be fixed by the capitalisation method *i.e.* by capitalising the value of the annual return from the land; and
(e) the determination of the value of the land solely on the basis of sale statistics may not give a realistic picture in many cases. The principle of capitalisation may be adopted and the value of land determined on this basis so as to counter-check the valuation made on the basis of sale statistics.

The method of determining the market value was further elaborated in the guidelines issued in 1979. It was pointed out that the market value has to be determined with reference to the price which a willing seller might have reasonably expected for similar property from a willing purchaser.

The amendment to the Constitution substituting the term 'amount' for 'compensation' and the connected court decisions have been referred to in Chapter 3. The full market value continues to be paid in view of the ruling of the courts. Moreover, the legal provisions enabling a person to make a reference to the civil court if he is not satisfied with the awards made by the Deputy Commissioner has invariably acted in favour of the land owner. The courts have generally been passing orders enhancing the compensation determined by the Land Acquisition Officers. **Table 7.3** shows the amount of compensation paid by the BDA in respect of four schemes and the enhanced amount awarded by the courts. The enhancement has ranged from about twice the amount originally awarded to eight times. In respect of Chandra Layout, while the BDA awarded Rs. 11,500 per acre, the court enhanced it by Rs. 94,000 resulting in a final payment of Rs. 1,06,400.

TABLE 7.3 : **Compensation paid by Bangalore Development Authority and enhanced by Court**

Rs./acre

Scheme	*Year of award*	*Compensation awarded*	*Enhanced by Court*	*Total compensation paid*
BTM	1978	17,986	35,820	53,806
Chandra layout	1979	11,500	94,900	1,06,400
Hennur Banasavadi	1982	28,750	79,950	1,08,700
Hennur Bellary Road I Stage	1986	49,450	84,160	1,33,610

The enhancement of compensation by courts has led to the comment that on the one hand, the Land Acquisition Officers are very conservative in the valuation of properties and on the other, the courts are very liberal. There seems to be some truth in both these contentions. One consequence of reference to courts is that the acquiring bodies are required to pay huge amounts long after the acquisition is over. By virtue of the amendment to the Land Acquisition Act in 1984, the rate of interest payment on the excess amount awarded by the court which was 5 per cent per annum has been revised to 9 per cent for a period of one year from the date of taking possession of land and 15 per cent for the subsequent period till the full amount is paid. The solatium charges (in consideration of the compulsory nature of acquisition) have also been increased from 15 to 30 per cent.

The inordinate delay in the process of acquisition has resulted in a shortfall in the land proposed to be acquired. Out of a total area of 18,643 acres notified by the BDA between 1976 and 1988, only an extent of 9,580 acres or about 50 per cent was actually acquired. Similarly, the Revenue Department could acquire 1,754 acres out of 4,604 acres notified from 1975 to 1988. Another consequence of such delay is that part of the area notified for acquisition is covered by unauthorised constructions, thus making a mockery of planned development.

In spite of the difficulties involved in acquiring land under the Land Acquisition Act, several acquiring bodies resort to this law in view of certain advantages, *viz;* land acquired is free from encumbrances and no stamp duty is payable.

LAND ACQUISITION BY CO-OPERATIVE HOUSE BUILDING SOCIETIES

A large number of House Building Co-operative Societies have been formed in and around Bangalore City. In 1977, there were 315 such societies with a membership of 1,05,474. By 1987, the number of societies had increased to 353, while the membership more than doubled to 2,30,586. These societies have been formed by workers in industrial undertakings, employees in government offices and quasi-government institutions like banks, weaker sections like slum dwellers, scheduled caste and tribes and by common people.

The co-operative societies have secured lands through two sources —direct purchase from land owners and through acquisition by the State Government. Lands are purchased from different types of persons "who may be categorized into agriculturists, speculators, estate agents and absentee landlords" (Mahadev and Boregowda, 1981), Mahadev and Boregowda have shown that speculators have sold more land than the others at the higher price of Rs. one lakh per hectare, while agriculturists could command only Rs. 64,000 per hectare Estate agents and absentee landlords have sold at higher rates than the agriculturists but lower than the speculators—Rs. 96,945 and Rs. 86,000 per hectare respectively.

Government, through the Revenue Department, has also acquired land under the Land Acquisition Act in favour of the House Building Co-operative Societies. As many as 128 housing societies were permitted to acquire lands through the Revenue department. The total area proposed for acquisition on behalf of these societies was to the extent of 11,200 acres. By the end of 1987, about 1,050 acres had been acquired.

After acquiring the land, the Societies have to develop it and get the layout plans approved by the BDA. From 1976 to 1986, the BDA gave approval to 97 layouts comprising 19,098 sites, whereas, the number of individual layouts approved was only 15 consisting of 467 sites (**Table 7.4**). Taking into account the approvals given by the City Improvement Trust Board (C.I.T.B.) (prior to 1976), the total number of sites formed by the Housing Societies up to 1986 comes to 30,003 in 182 layouts.

TABLE 7.4 : **Layouts approved by BDA and Number of Sites formed (Housing Societies and Private Layouts)**

Year	*Layouts of societies approved*	*No. of sites formed by societies*	*Individual layouts approved*	*No. of sites formed*	*Total No. of layouts*	*Total No. of sites formed*
1976	9	2,379	2	33	11	2,412
1977	9	566	2	15	11	581
1978	4	788	—	—	4	788
1979	5	876	1	57	6	933
1980	8	467	3	102	11	569
1981	10	2,081	1	11	11	2,092
1982	8	642	2	118	10	760
1983	15	3,443	4	131	19	3,574
1984	11	3,849	—	—	11	3,849
1985	10	1,391	—	—	10	1,391
1986	8	2,616	—	—	8	2,616
Total	97	19,098	15	467	112	19,565

The large scale acquisition of land by the Housing Societies, while helping to mitigate the housing problem, has also had some adverse consequences. The Government noticed that the purchases of land directly from the land owners not in accordance with law providing for acquisition of land resulted in uncontrolled, unplanned and haphazard growth of the city of Bangalore. Most of the societies operate in the rural-urban fringe and in the interior, where provision of infrastructure and civic amenities becomes both costly and difficult. "Most of the developments by the co-operative societies are not found on major highways radiating from out of the city but only in the interstitial areas and minor roads. This is mainly because most of the land along the highways have already been developed by industries since the accessibility is at a premium . . . . . Hence, the residential areas have been pushed into the interior both because of non-availability of space as well as high land value along the developed highways" (Mahadev and Boregowda, 1981). It was also observed that such developments led to acute problems with regard to provision of water, transport facilities and other civic amenities. In order to place some restrictions on the activities of these societies, Government took the following decisions in June 1985 :

(i) the Revenue Department (of the State Government) shall not acquire any more land in the Bangalore Metropolitan Area for housing co-operative societies. Such societies would have to approach the BDA for their requirements of land and the BDA shall be the only agency to acquire land for housing purposes in the Bangalore Metropolitan Area.

(ii) all transactions of land in Bangalore metropolitan area to housing societies should be frozen. Conversion of agricultural land in favour of such societies must be prohibited;

(iii) the extent of land to be allotted by the BDA to a single housing society must be limited to 20 acres.

In respect of 69 societies where acquisition proceedings had been initiated, they were permitted to complete the acquisition proceedings subject to clearance given by the Three Member Committee comprising the Registrar of Co-operative Societies as Chairman, the Secretary, BDA and the Special Deputy Commissioner, Bangalore (Revenue), Bangalore District, as members. This Committee was expected to scrutinise the proposals of the societies with reference to membership, mainly with a view to checking the bogus membership. There was also criticism that a number of members of the societies already owned plots or houses. Another 49 societies were added for acquisition of land in 1986. Thus a total of 128 societies have been permitted to acquire lands subject to verification by the Three Member Committee. Although the cut off date for registration of the societies was fixed as 30th June, 1984 initially, fresh membership was permitted by an order in 1987 subject to the condition that the agreement for purchase of lands should have been entered into prior to 30th June, 1984. Certain other relaxations were also extended to the societies. The following are worth noting:

(a) in case the lands proposed for acquisition for societies fall in the green belt, individual cases may be examined by Government for taking a decision;

(b) exemption under the Urban Land Ceiling Act and the Land Reforms Act may be given in favour of the societies in conformity with the provisions of both the laws;

(c) the Bangalore Water Supply and Sewerage Board (BWSSB) should make arrangements for supply of water and sewerage facilities to these societies on payment of necessary funds.

The activities of the housing societies and the policy adopted by Government towards these societies raise a number of questions. In the first place, the societies have undoubtedly played a useful role in adding to the housing stock in the city. They have acquired and developed about

10 sq. km. of space. To that extent, they have contributed in mitigating the housing shortage in Bangalore. Secondly, they have helped in mobilization of private capital for housing development. The individual members obtain funds for construction by way of loan either from the organisation in which they are employed or from other private sources. At the same time, the functioning of some of these societies has given rise to misapprehension in the minds of the public. The complaints relate mainly to bogus membership, bogus agreements with the landlords and irregularities in distribution of sites. Such malpractices defeats the purpose of equitable distribution for which co-operative societies are formed. Procurement of a site through the society thus becomes a means of speculation rather than a means to genuine ownership of a dwelling.

While it is necessary to encourage the co-operative movement in the housing sector, it is also essential to streamline the procedure for acquisition of land for these societies. The normal practice seems to be that the societies first enter into agreements with land-owners and then approach Government for acquisition. This is done without reference to the land use proposals in the Development Plan and in violation of laws relating to Land Reforms, Urban Land Ceiling and Town and Country Planning. All this results not only in delay in acquisition but additional costs and uncertainty. It is, therefore, desirable to have a single public agency to acquire land for housing and other public purposes in the Bangalore Metropolitan Area. Housing societies can approach this agency for their land acquisition.

LAND ACQUISITION UNDER THE URBAN LAND CEILING ACT

The Urban Land Ceiling and Regulation Act provides for the acquisition of vacant land in excess of the ceiling limit imposed under the law. Under the Act, Bangalore Urban Agglomeration is included in 'B' category where the ceiling limit is fixed at 1,000 sq. metres of vacant land. The year-wise particulars relating to the excess area determined and acquired in the Bangalore Urban Agglomeration may be seen in Table 7.5. Totally, an area of 77,458 acres of land has been declared by the owners under Section 6 of the Urban Land Ceiling Act till the end of 1987. Out of this, an extent of 11,321 acres was determined as excess land by the competent authorities. The area acquired finally under the Act was to the extent of 3,445 acres. Thus, only about 14 per cent of the area declared as excess by the land owners was actually determined as excess by the competent authorities and a meagre 4 per cent acquired. Again, the land acquired out of the excess determined accounts for only about 31 per cent.

TABLE 7.5 : **Land acquired under Urban Land (Ceiling and Regulation) Act in BangaloreUrban Agglomeration**

(acres)

Year	*Excees vacant land declared under Section 8(i)*	*Excess land determined by compe-tent authority*	*Area acquired*
1976	43,949	8	—
1977	21,813	1,162	5
1978	985	821	3
1979	2,447	756	13
1980	1,691	1,093	8
1981	940	1,361	93
1982	339	928	45
1983	1,541	1.043	57
1984	1,721	1,969	1,412
1985	1,646	1,559	1,408
1986	250	406	311
1987	226	171	90
Total	77,548	11,275	3,445

An analysis of the implementation of the Urban Land Ceiling Act in Bangalore reveals the following :

(a) The provision relating to grant of exemption has been made use of liberally. Under Section 20 of the Urban Land Ceiling Act, a person can be permitted to hold land in excess of the ceiling limit on grounds of hardship or in the public interest. The statement showing the details of land exempted for various purposes can be seen in Table 7.6. Totally, 6,521 acres of land have been exempted from the provisions of the Urban Land Ceiling Act up to 1987. The maximum area exempted *i.e.* over 50 per cent is for industrial purpose, followod by hardship cases to the extent of about 25 per cent and agricultural purpose accounting for nearly 12 per cent.

(b) The State Government has constituted two committees to examine and decide on the allocation of surplus land acquired — one, to consider the allotment of land to government departments and agencies to meet their requirements, and another, to consider allotment for housing and other purposes. The excess land allocated so far to various organisations is 345 acres *i.e.* about 10 per cent of the area acquired.

TABLE 7.6 : **Exemption granted under Urban Land (Ceiling and Regulation) Act in Bangalore Urban Agglomeration from 1976 to 1987)**

Purpose	*No. of cases*	*Extent (acres)*
Agriculture	315	753
Industrial	1,625	3,585
Residential	135	139
Hardship	289	1,640
Stud Farm	3	310
Group Housing	10	94
Total	2,375	6,521

(c) Section 21 of the Act empowers the competent authority to permit a person to hold excess land for the purpose of construction of dwelling units or accommodation for the weaker sections of society. Each dwelling unit in such a plan should not exceed 80 sq.metres. Not a single person seems to have come forward to make use of this provision. This also reflects the attitude of the land owning class towards the weaker sections. It is to be noted that Government has also not come forward with large scale projects to accommodate the poorer sections on the surplus lands acquired.

(d) Location-wise, the excess land 'acquired by government are mostly in the periphery and interior areas. Much of the prime land within the city and its vicinity has been granted exemption. Thus valuable land which could have been utilised for public purposes and for housing and weaker sections in the city has been lost for private and commercial purposes'.

(e) Section 22 of the Act empowers the competent authority to permit holding of the land after demolition of the existing building for utilising it for the purpose of re-development in accordance with the Master Plan. In Bangalore, there are a number of bungalows covering vast extent of appurtenant land. Some of these bungalows were constructed during the British times and in the early years of independence. Once the buildings are demolished, a lot of vacant land would become available. However, a number of owners are using this provision of re-development for putting up multistoreyed buildings. Although residential buildings may help in adding to the housing stock, most of these have turned out to be commercial ventures providing flats for the well-to-do sections of the society. In some cases, the land used is also got changed for commercial purposes where the profit motive predominates.

(f) One of the principal aims of the Act was to control the spiralling prices of urban land. This has not been achieved. On the other hand, the land values have been rising in Bangalore even after 1976 when the Act came into force, as already noted in a previous chapter.

(g) According to Sections 26 and 27 of the Act, whenever a vacant land or a building is to be sold, the competent authority is to be notified and the State Government has a pre-emptive right to purchase such property. The right of first option of purchase of property made available to Government has, however, hardly been exercised.

(h) Although a ceiling has been imposed on the plinth area of a dwelling unit (300 sq. metres), this has not been incorporated in the Building Byelaws for Bangalore. As such, one sees any number of huge houses in excess of the ceiling limit coming up and no legal action is taken in such cases.

On the whole, the objectives of the law relating to Urban Land Ceiling have not been achieved in Bangalore. The excess land acquired is meagre and does not enjoy locational advantage. The land prices have not been controlled and the land made available to the weaker sections is negligible, thus defeating the purpose of equitable distribution.

LAND DISPOSAL POLICY

The ultimate aim of land acquisition is allocation of the land for the purpose for which it is acquired. A public authority is also expected to ensure that the distribution of land is efficient and equitable. The policy adopted by the BDA in the distribution of land is examined below:

No clear policy has been laid down by the BDA or the Government in the matter of land distribution. However, the Bangalore Development Authority (Allotment of Sites) Rules, 1984 and some of the decisions taken from time to time reveal certain policy measures.

Methods of Land Disposal

After a layout is developed, land is allocated for different uses broadly as follows : *(i)* residential sites - 50 per cent, and *(ii)* infrastructure like roads, drains and other civic amenities - 50 per cent. The BDA Act was amended in 1984 to provide for reservation for public parks and playgrounds at a minimum of 15 per cent and for civic amenities at a minimum of 10 per cent of the total area of the layout. In order to prevent diversion of land for other purposes, the Amendment Act of 1984 prohibited the use of an area reserved for parks, playgrounds and civic amenities for other purposes and made any such disposal of the reserved areas null and void. These provisions are significant from the point of view of land use control.

Basically, two methods are followed in disposal of land, *viz.*, lease-*cum*-sale and auction. The following conditions govern the allotment of a site on lease-*cum*-sale basis. The allottee shall :

(a) construct the building on the site in accordance with the plan approved by the BDA;
(b) execute a lease-*cum*-sale agreement and get it registered within 45 days;
(c) construct the building within a period of three years from the date of execution of the agreement failing which the agreement is liable to be revoked and the allottee evicted;
(d) get the sale deed of the site executed after a period of ten years from the date of the lease-*cum*-sale agreement; and
(e) the allottee shall not alienate the site or the building constructed on it within a period of ten years, except, by way of mortgage in favour of government or certain financial institutions for the construction of the building. The BDA can resume the site if there conditions are violated.

All sites which are earmarked for commercial uses and residential sites which are corner sites *i.e.* a site situated at the intersection of two streets or roads are to be sold by public auction. This is done mainly with a view to augment the revenues of the BDA. The price fetched by way of sale of sites in auctions has been brought out while discussing land values in Chapter 5.

Land Distribution

The distribution of sites is governed by a policy of reservations whose features are as follows :

(a) Thirty per cent of the total number of sites in the layout is reserved for persons belonging to economically weaker sections at 50 per cent of the value of the sites. A person is said to belong to 'economically weaker section' if his total annual income including that of any member of his family does not exceed Rs. 6,000. and

(b) The sites in any layout are to be allotted to different categories of the community as indicated below:

(a) Backward Tribes	2%
(b) Scheduled Tribes	3%
(c) Scheduled Castes	13%
(d) Members of the Armed Forces of the Union, Ex-servicemen and members of the families of the deceased servicemen	5%
(e) State Government employees	10%
(f) Employees of the Central Government and public sector undertakings and statutory bodies owned or controlled by the State Government or the Central Government	8%
(g) Physically handicapped persons	2%
(i) General public	52%
(j) To be allotted at the discretion of the Authority with preference being given to persons who have outstanding achievements in the arts, science or sports or any other field	5%

No fixed criteria have been laid down for the selection of applicants for the allotment of sites. The rule only mentions that 'the authority shall consider the case of each application on its merits and having regard to the following principles':

(i) the income of the applicant and his capacity to purchase a site and build a house thereon (this is not applicable to SCs/STs/BTs).

(ii) the status of the applicant—whether he is married or single and had dependent children;
(iii) the number of times the applicant had applied for allotment of a site but could not secure a site earlier;
(iv) the fact of the applicant's land having been acquired for the formation of the layout.

In practice, the main consideration guiding selection is the number of times a person has attempted to secure a site. Any applicant should, however, satisfy the following eligibility conditions :

(i) he should be a domicile of Karnataka for not less than ten years prior to the date of registration; and
(ii) he or his family members should not own a site or a house within the Bangalore Metropolitan Area. The conditions of domicile may be relaxed in certain circumstances like the person serving in the armed forces or having gone out of the State for employment.

Allotment of stray sites are governed by the following criteria :

(a) disposal by auction	50%
(b) freedom fighters who are residents of Bangalore for not less than ten years	5%
(c) persons who have won recognition in the field of arts, science, literature etc.,	25%
(d) voluntary and service organisations	20%

Since its inception in 1976, the BDA distributed 41,922 sites till 1986-87 *i.e.* in a period of ten years. Prior to that, the CITB had distributed 64,656 sites from 1945 to 1976 *i.e.* in a period of about 30 years. So totally, 1,06,576 sites have been distributed by the premier Development Authority of Bangalore, over a period of roughly 40 years. The year-wise distribution of sites from 1976-77 is given in Table 7.7. The period of three years from 1979-80 to 1981-82 has recorded a very poor performance—just 1,153 sites, the year 1980-81 showing a blank. The years 1976-78 witnessed a good achievement of about 23,000 sites. Thereafter, the performance has not been up to the mark.

The BDA has constructed totally 7,269 houses involving a total project cost of nearly Rs. 92 crore. The details of housing schemes taken up by the BDA are given in Table 7.8. Houses constructed for the economically weaker sections (2,792) constitute 38 per cent, while the low income group (2,498) accounts for a little over a third of the total. As many as 2,484 houses have been constructed under the self-financing scheme (in Rajamahal Vilas II Stage, Nandini and BTM layouts).

TABLE 7.7 : **Allotment of Sites by the Bangalore Development Authority**

Year	*No. of sites allotted*
1976-77	12,270
1977-78	10,764
1978-79	4,050
1979-80	450
1980-81	—
1981-82	703
1982-83	2,000
1983-84	1,403
1984-85	5,836
1985-86	1,834
1986-87	2,612
	41,922
Number of sites allotted by CITB from 1945 to 1976	64,656
Total	1,06,578

Source : Bangalore Development Authority.

TABLE 7.8 : **Houses constructed by Bangalore Development Authority**

Location	*EWS*	*LIG*	*MIG*	*HIG*	*Total*
Austin Town I Stage	228	448	90	—	766
II Stage	156	432	72	—	660
III Stage	—	193	30	—	223
Kallahalli I & II Stage	32	128	146	30	336
Domlur II, III and IV Stage	376	317	107	—	800
Kumaraswamy I Stage	1,000	—	—	—	1,000
Kumaraswamy II Stage	1,000	—	—	—	1,000
Rajmahal Vilas II Stage	—	—	—	558	558
BTM	—	220	288	—	508
Nandini	—	760	658	—	1,418
Total	2,792	2,498	1,391	588	7,269

EWS : Economically Weaker Sections
LIG : Low Income Group
MIG : Middle Income Group
HIG : High Income Group

Source : Bangalore Development Authority.

The development norms adopted by BDA appear to be liberal. Only 50 per cent of the land in a layout is utilised for formation of sites, the remaining half being used for infrastructural facilities and civic amenities. The number of individual sites formed per acre is only 10. Secondly, the plot sizes have tended to be generous, some of them being as large as 60′ × 90′ and 80′ × 120′. Though allotment of such large size plots has now been given up, the present maximum size of 50′ × 80′ must be considered a luxury in the context of the demand for urban land; it is also uneconomical utilisation of land.

Another vital problem relates to the pricing of land. For any particular project, the BDA provides land at cost (including cost of acquisition, development and creation of amenities) plus a margin resulting in a surplus of about 5 per cent, after meeting all its other expenses. Although the bigger sites are priced higher, the land supplied by BDA is far cheaper than the market value. A number of institutions, ostensibly championing public causes, have been the beneficiaries of large pieces of land at low prices. Thus cheap land made available by public authorities like BDA has led to inefficient and uneconomical use of land. It has also resulted in speculative practices as it is observed that a number of allotees keep their sites vacant for years together with a view to profit from the rising prices. The BDA has obviously failed to enforce the condition pertaining to construction of the house within a period of three years from the date of allotment of the site.

Providing access to shelter to the poor and disadvantaged sections of the community has been a major plank in the policy of the public authorities in Bangalore. As already noted, the BDA is expected to earmark 30 per cent of the sites in any layout it develops to the economically weaker sections. Out of the 41,922 sites distributed by the BDA from 1976-77 to 1986-87, the number of sites allotted to the weaker sections is 12,356. This accounts for 30 per cent of the total sites and conforms to the policy laid down. Similarly, out of the houses constructed by BDA (**Table 7.8**), 38 per cent has been earmarked for economically weaker sections.

Land for the Poor

Land issues become crucial while dealing with the problem of the urban poor and slums in any growing city. It is estimated that there are about 400 slums in Bangalore with a population of about 350,000.

The policy adopted by the government towards slums is three-fold :

(a) on-site improvement;
(b) resettlement in new area; and
(c) eviction.

The first measure known as the "environmental improvement of slums" comprises provision of basic amenities like water, roads, drains, etc., in the place where the slum has developed. This scheme has been taken up on a large scale and most of the slums in Bangalore have been provided with some minimum facilities. The second alternative of shifting the slum-dwellers and resettling them in new place by providing them sites and service or constructing new houses has been tried in some cases. A notable example of resettlement is the Lingarajapuram case — about 1,200 families settled in the Miller Tank bed area were shifted to Lingarajapuram near the outskirts of the city by the Corporation and were provided sites by the BDA.

Eviction of slum dwellers has also been resorted to by the authorities in Bangalore at different points of time. Large scale evictions were made in 1985 which resulted in massive demonstrations against demolition of slum settlements. A national seminar on Housing for the urban poor organised by the Karnataka Kolageri Nivasigala Samyukta Sanghatana in October 1985[2] issued a statement pointing out that "the crucial issue of the right to use the land" has, as yet been entirely unresolved in the ongoing struggles in which the poor are constantly on the defensive. The enormous commercialisation and speculation in land has marginalised vast sections of the population and has made rational planning processes virtually impossible." The statement also contended that it was necessary to question the "public purpose" for which slum eviction was often carried out and argued that vast stretches of prime land held by public and charitable institutions for private purposes could be used for housing the urban poor. It is interesting to note that the Supreme Court in its historic judgement of July 10, 1985 in the Bombay Pavement and Slum Dwellers Case[3] while acknowledging that the right to life guaranteed in Article 21 of the Constitution cannot be separated from the right to livelihood, nevertheless, endorsed evictions.

Grant or Lease of Land

It is necessary to refer to the system of grant or long term lease of land sometimes extending up to 99 years. The Karnataka Land Revenue Act provides for grant or lease of land to persons for the purpose of agriculture or for certain non-agricultural purposes. The Karnataka Municipal Corporation Act also empowers the Corporation authorities to lease land to individuals or institutions within their jurisdiction.

Under the Land Revenue Act, the Deputy Commissioner of Bangalore District has leased out land in the fringe areas and rural parts of the metropolitan region. During the period 1975-76 to 1985-86, an area of 2,488 acres has been granted on lease in Bangalore North and South Taluks (**Table 7.9**). Bulk of the land *i.e.* 2,222 acres has been granted for agricultural purpose and of the remaining 266 acres, 45 acres are allotted for educational purposes, *i.e.* setting up educational institutions. Land is granted usually at an upset price. This is very nominal ranging from Rs. 50 to a few thousands. Sometimes the upset price is waived, supposedly in deserving cases where the person concerned is very poor and unable to pay any price.

TABLE 7.9 : **Land granted/leased in Bangalore North and South Taluks by Deputy Commissioner (in acres)**

Year	*Agricultural Purpose*	*Non-agricultural Purposes*	*Total*
1975-76	21	37	58
1976-77	30	6	36
1977-78	202	62	264
1978-79	796	9	805
1979-80	347	30	377
1980-81	124	46	170
1981-82	161	41	202
1982-83	76	1	77
1983-84	10	29	39
1984-85	445	5	450
1985-86	10	—	10
Total	2,222	266	2,488

The City Corporation has been granting lease of lands for various purposes—setting up schools, hospitals, hostels, house sites, shops etc. Records pertaining to the lands given by the Municipal Council or Government within the municipal area of Bangalore pertaining to the early part of this century make interesting reading. There is a statement showing such lands given to private persons or bodies from 1882 till 1917. One of the earliest grants was made on 29th March 1884 covering an extent of 18 acres to the east of the Municipal City Office in favour of Lady Superior, St. Martha's Hospital for the purpose of constructing a free hospital for public use. Certain other important grants made during that period are given in **Table 7.10**. The basis on which the land value was fixed is not known. It is interesting to observe that while the Century Club and Cosmopolitan Club have been given land free of cost, institutions doing humanitarian work like Ramakrishna Mission and Sringeri Mutt have been made to pay a price.

A number of sites in different parts of the city have been leased out to different individuals and institutions. As on 1.10.1984, nearly 60 acres of land have been leased by the Corporation in favour of 2,655 parties - 631 in favour of individuals and the remaining 2,024 pertaining to allotment of bulk sites. The bulk allotments include land for the weaker sections for house sites (in places like Harijan Colony, Marenahalli, Magadi Road I Cross, Jayanagar 9th Block etc.).

The Corporation does not have any policy of disposal of lands either by way of lease or sale. Lot of valuable land within the city has been given away at nominal rates and this has resulted in inefficient utilisation of valuable land at prime locations in the city, and loss of revenue. Such adhoc policy of leasing out lands must be given up.

NEW APPROACHES TO ACQUISITION AND DISPOSAL

An evaluation of the policies pursued so far by the public authorities in the matter of acquisition, development and disposal of land leads to the following conclusions :

(a) the process of acquisition of land under the Land Acquisition Act for the purpose of housing and other public purposes is, by and large, slow, lengthy and cumbersome;

(b) acquisition of land for industrial purposes under the Karnataka Industrial Area Development Board Act, through negotiation has been speedy and free from many of the hurdles faced under the Land Acquisition Act;

(c) public policy, though aimed at providing land and housing to the weaker sections and low income groups, is not fully oriented to implement it to the desired extent;

(d) the co-operative sector has made a useful contribution to housing development but its Land Acquisition Policy has led to haphazard growth of the city;

(e) delays in acquisition and development of land have led to unauthorised constructions, and squatting;

TABLE 7.10 : **Land granted/leased by Bangalore City Corporation**

Name of Grantee/lessee	*Area and Location (acres)*	*Purpose*	*Date of allotment*	*Value*
Board of Directors, YMCA, Bangalore	5.34 - East of the leading from Cenotaph Road to the Revenue Survey Office	For constructing a building in which provision would be made for a library, reading room, literature hall, classrooms, hostel and tennis court, athletics ground etc.	22.4.1915	Free Grant
Janopakari Doddanna Chetty	3.30 - Near the North Fort Gate	For constructing a free Anglo Vernacular School	27.9.1902	Free Grant
Vokkaligara Sangha	12.10 South of Koracharapalya and East of the Fort	For establishing a printing press, erecting a hostel for students and other buildings and forming ornamental park or flower garden	29.3.1909	Free Grant
President, Ramakrishna Mission	3.10 and 1.7-Bull Temple Road	For building the Ramakrishna Mission Institute	6.9.1907 and 1.8.84	Rs. 325 and Rs.118
Sri Sringeri Mutt	15.32 Shankarapuram Extension	For constructing Shankar Mutt building/ Quarters for the Indian Sanskrit Students	27.9.1907 and 6.1.1910	Rs.7048
Cosmopolitan Club	8 - Adjoining Tennis Court in Cubbon Park	For constructing a building for Cosmopolitan Club, Bangalore	13.5.1915	Free Grant
Century Club	9.3-Behind the Revenue Survey Office in Cubbon Park	Erecting a building for the club	16.11.1916 and 22.3.1917	Free Grant

Source : Bangalore City Corporation records.

(f) the Urban Land Ceiling Law has not had the desired effect either in controlling rise in land values or in the matter of equitable distribution of land;

(g) the distribution and use of land has not been efficient.

It is, therefore, necessary to reshape the Land Acquisition Policy in keeping with the objectives of Land Use Policy. The following approaches are suggested.

Innovative Techniques of Acquisition

(i) *Land Banking :* Substantial extent of land is acquired well in advance of the need, and land is released in stages, as and when required for various development activities. The chief benefit of advance acquisition is to preserve the sites best suited for future public purposes from premature commitment to private use (Shoup and Mack, 1968). The main difficulty in adopting the banking system is the requirement of huge funds to undertake acquisition on a large scale. This system has been practised with success in countries like Netherlands and Sweden.

(ii) *Land Pooling :* This is a technique whereby small pieces of raw lands are assembled and consolidated by the public authority without paying actual cash compensation to owners. The authorities will service the land, subdivide it according to planned schemes and reconvey part of the serviced land to the owners. The remaining land is sold to the public to recover the development charges and other expenses. A modified form of land pooling consists in reconveying only one to three building sites to each of the land owners who contributed to the pool and sell the remaining sites to the public. Out of the sale proceeds, the land owners are compensated in proportion to their land contribution to the pool after meeting the costs of planning and development.

This system has several merits. Both the land owners and the public authorities stand to gain. The land owner is not fully deprived of his land and the compensation in land may even work out to be more than monetary compensation. So far as the public authority is concerned, this method enables quicker implementation of a project with the cooperation of the land owners and the sale of retained land also helps to meet the cost of development. It is, therefore, suited to countries where governments find it difficult to finance public infrastructure investment (Shoup, 1983). This method has been tried in countries like South Korea, Taiwan and Australia and in some States in India like Gujarat.

(iii) *Excess Acquisition :* In this method, land in excess of the requirements is acquired around the project site. This is a means of regulating the development that is attracted by availability of infrastructure. In a project area, it enables the public authority to hold the excess land for future use or dispose it of at a profit and use the additional funds for cross-subsidy purposes.

This technique has been adopted in Toronto in Canada in the course of construction of the sub-way system. The Sub-way Authority acquired more lands than necessary at the station entrance and this excess land was leased to private developers for 55 years. These developers had to submit proposals compatible with sub-way facility. Such a system would involve heavy investments initially. It would, however, be suitable while tackling large scale projects such as the Bangalore Rapid Rail Transit System.

(iv) *Guided Development :* Under this scheme, selected private developers are made responsible for land assembly and services. The Development Authority will frame guidelines stipulating space norms. This technique is aimed at ensuring a fair return on investment to the private owner or developer and the availability of a relatively large proportion of serviced land for allotment to low income families at affordable prices. Plots for middle and higher income groups and for certain non-residential uses can also be included in the scheme. The Development Authority will have to provide the essential offside infrastructure like access to roads, water supply, etc. This scheme is being tried in Tamil Nadu under the Urban Development Project aided by the World Bank.

The above techniques can help in overcoming delays in acquisition and also in better Land Use Planning.

Urban Land Ceiling

The National Commission on Urbanisation (NCU) has suggested that the Urban Land Ceiling Act must be 'rationalised and made easy of implementation'. Recommendations include deletion of the provision relating to discretionary exemptions and providing moratorium of five years to the land owner for development of the vacant land. However, in the case of Bangalore, nothing positive is likely to come out at this stage —more than 14 years after the Act came into force—even if the law is rationalised. Much of the prime land in the city has been exempted from the provisions of the Act and the process of granting exemption, irrespective of the merits of the case, continues unabated. Certain legal anomalies and ambiguities persist. The land owners find ingenious ways to overcome the clutches of law, sometimes with the connivance of the powers that be and sometimes with the help of the courts. It would, therefore, be far better if this law is removed from the statute book. This may help in quicker releases of land in the land market and possibly have a softening influence on the high land prices.

Shift in Bias Towards Weaker Sections

In land distribution, the crucial issue to be resolved is the target groups. The section of the population that needs the assistance and support of government for shelter belongs mostly to the poor and low income groups. The benefits of the efforts of the public authorities have, however, been reaped in a large measure by the middle and high income groups. BDA's policy of reserving 30 per cent of the sites in a layout to the weaker sections needs to be revised. Atleast 50 per cent of the sites should go to the lower income categories. The remaining 50 per cent can be provided to the middle and higher income groups in order to cross-subsidise the costs towards the poorer sections. Further, the plot size of 15 sq.mtrs. now given to the poor is far too low for any dignified human living and must be raised to 30 sq.mtrs. Provision of access to housing at affordable prices is a basic aim of Land Use Policy and will help preventing squatting. "A continuation of public subsidy is unescapable if the accessibility of the poor to land and shelter is to be improved. The only unsubsidised affordable alternatives are the slums in the city and unauthorised settlement in the green belt" (Town and Country Planning Organisation Delhi, 1988).

Coordination of Land Accquisition and Land Use Policies

Land acquisition should take place not in isolation but in coordination with Land Use Policy. Acquisition programmes must conform to the proposals in the Land Use Plan. Land earmarked for uses like open spaces parks, recreation should not be acquired for other development purposes. In view of past experience in Bangalore, acquisition of land in the green belt must be avoided. Decision on the location of projects and the quantity of land to be acquired must be guided by considerations of efficiency and economy in the use of land. This is important to ensure maximum return on the public investments made in acquiring and developing the land. Feasibility studies which would include site selection criteria, cost-benefit analysis and estimating market trends, must precede the undertaking of an acquisition project. It is observed that there is a time lag between acquisition and utilisation of land. There are instances where land handed over to the allottees has remained unutilised for years together. This is mainly on account of non-provision of amenities like water supply and drainage at the project site in time. It is, therefore, essential to ensure co-ordination between BDA or the acquiring authority and other agencies like Water Supply Board, Electricity Board etc., so that building activity takes place without delay.

NOTES

1. A stray site is defined as 'Site which was once allotted but subsequently the allotment was either cancelled or surrendered by the allottee or a site which has been formed on account of readjustment in the plan subsequent to the issue of notifications inviting applications for allotment of sites'.
2. Karnataka Slum Dwellers' United Organisation.
3. Olga Tellis and others *vs.* The Bombay Municipal Corporation.

8

FISCAL POLICIES

One form of government intervention in the urban land market can be through fiscal measures or taxation of Urban Land Property. Although taxes are generally meant to raise revenues, they can also serve as a significant tool to influence Land Use Policy and help achieve the objectives of efficiency in resource allocation and equity in distribution. The objectives of fiscal policies in the context of Urban Land Policy can be stated as follows:

(i) to provide general revenue, especially for local government;
(ii) to provide revenue to finance expenditure on specified public services;
(iii) to provide incentives for efficient allocation of resources in the Urban Land Market; and
(iv) to reduce inequities in the distribution of land ownership, land income or benefits of land use (World Bank, 1978).

LAND TAX SYSTEMS

Different types of land tax systems have been developed over the years and adopted in different countries. The important systems are the following:

1. Site Value Taxation or Land Value System;
2. General Property Taxation;
3. Betterment Levies.

Land Value System

Land value (or site value) tax is levied on the value of the land and is considered particularly significant in the context of rising land values. Higher land taxes are expected to reduce the market value of the land. Vacant land or underutilised land, when taxed at a rate that escalates with the length of time for which the land is held idle, will have the effect of discouraging speculation and prevent exorbitant rise in land prices. Secondly, such a tax on vacant land can stimulate building activity and add to the housing or building stock. The value of land also depends on the public services provided and the land owner would be under pressure to develop already serviced land. Site value tax forces land utilisation to the maximum limit as the tax will increase with increase in economic rent of land (Dale Bails, 1974). It is also expected that taxation on the basis of land value would promote the use of land for the purpose for which it has been zoned. Another argument in favour of land value tax is that it captures betterment. Any increase in the value of land results in an increase in the annual tax liability. As the burden of tax is borne by the land owners, it also helps in achieving equity, especially where land is concentrated in higher income groups.

Land value tax is criticised on the ground that "there is no meaningful way, in theory as well as in practice, of separating the value of the site from the value of improvements if the site is not a vacant one" (Netzer, 1966). It is argued that it is the improvement on the land, by altering the character of the location, which changes the site value. It becomes difficult to determine the value of the land once it is built upon. Secondly, while a tax on vacant land may stimulate development, it may not be desirable to encourage immediate development of all urban land. Some land may have to be held to meet the requirements of future development. On the whole, at least theoretically, land value tax is expected to reduce land prices. "Imposition of site value taxation would then encourage an increased rate of investment in new buildings, less speculation and more intensive use of land" (Rakesh Mohan, 1987).

Property Tax

Property tax is a levy on property which includes land and buildings. The basis of assessment is the capital value or the annual rental value of the property. In India, which has followed the British system, the latter method is commonly used whereas in a country like the United States, the former is in vogue. In other words, the legal base of the tax in the United States is the market value of the property *i.e.* a tax rate is applied to a measure of the stock of capital. In India the flow of rental income from the stock is the tax base (Schroeder, 1980).

The annual rental value is defined as the gross annual rent at which the property may reasonably be expected to be let from year to year. It is not the actual rent but a hypothetical value. The methods of assessment and the rate structure may vary from place to place. Tax can be levied on a flat rate basis or on a progressive scale. A number of problems arise in administrating the annual rent based system. In the first place, there are no uniform methods of property valuation. This along with the absence of trained persons, renders valuation subjective and arbitrary. Secondly, the rental value fails to take into account the rise in property values. As the city develops, the true value may go on rising although the rent might have been fixed long ago (Ursula Hicks, 1961). While reassessment at periodic intervals may be legally possible, this is severely limited by the operation of Rent Control Laws in India. The court rulings have supported the concept of 'fair rent' as determined under Rent Control Acts irrespective of whether the fair rent has been determined by a Rent Control Court or not. This interpretation has also restricted the scope of local authorities to increase its revenues through the property tax. Although a progressive rate structure is expected to promote equity in the tax system, paucity or accurate rental evidence often results in undervaluation and thus dilutes the principle of equity.

The capital value system has been criticised on the ground that it is more difficult to assess as it involves technical details. Secondly, it is influenced by cyclical fluctuations, going up in a period of prosperity and coming down during depression. And thus capital values tend to reflect the oscillations of the cycle and are less accurate as a basis for levying property taxes than the current income or rental value of property.

Betterment Levy

Tax on property based on annual rental or capital value, it is argued, captures only a small part of betterment as assessed values are much lower than market prices. Hence, a separate tax can be levied on betterment or the benefits arising from development or provision of public services. Levy on betterment can be of the following types :

(i) a levy can be imposed whenever some development takes place on a piece of land;

(ii) a betterment fee can be levied when there is a change in land use or conversion from agriculture to non-agricultural use;

(iii) land value increase can be taxed when the ownership of property is transferred; and

(iv) a special levy can be imposed on the betterment caused by investment in order to finance a site specific Public Investment Project. The property can be assessed before the project is undertaken based on the increase in the total property value likely to accrue as a result of the investment. Project costs can be apportioned to items like land area.

Betterment levies can serve as an effective instrument of land policy. A tax levied on a change of land use can influence the Land Use Planning process. Betterment levis particularly useful in financing public investment. The unwillingness or inability on the part of government in developing countries to recover the costs of public services can be overcome by taxing the gain in land value, whenever, services are provided. "The tax effectively takes the place of a price for services" (Shoup, 1983). The argument against betterment levy is that there is an element of uncertainty in future betterment as the amount of improvement and the time it would take to effect that improvement are not exactly known. There is also a degree of inequity in the levy as the low income people may be unwilling or unable to pay for a particular public benefit which may actually help the higher income groups whose land may gain in value. Finally, it is observed that this levy has not proved to be a good source of revenue. Grimes (1974), after examining the operation of the system in a number of countries concluded that receipts from betterment levies and land value increment taxes were low compared with receipts from property taxes and other revenue sources.

The tax system relating to land and property in Bangalore are discussed below:

TAXATION OF URBAN LAND AND PROPERTY IN BANGALORE

The different taxes levied on Urban Land and Property in Bangalore are the following :

(a) Property Tax ;
(b) Tax on Vacant Land ;
(c) Betterment Fee ; and
(d) Stamp Duty and Registration Charges.

Property Tax

For Bangalore city, property tax is levied under the Karnataka Municipal Corporation Act, 1976. The tax is levied on all buildings and lands situated in the Corporation area and also in the layouts developed by the Bangalore Development Authority. In the areas under the jurisdiction of the BDA, tax is levied on the same lines as in the Corporation area.

Assessment: The assessment of property tax is based on the annual rental value of the property. The method of assessment is described in section 109 of the Karnataka Municipal Corporation Act. The rateable value of a land or a building will be the gross annual rent at which the buildings or land is reasonably expected to let from month to month or from year to year at the time of assessment. Deduction to the extent of 16.66 per cent is made towards allowances for repairs of the building. In the case of a building not ordinarily let out and where the gross annual rent cannot be estimated, the rateable value is deemed to be 6 per cent of the estimated market cost of erecting the building. A minimum of 10% of the cost is deductible towards depreciation.

Rate Structure : According to the Karnataka Municipal Corporation Act, property tax is to be levied at not less than 20 per cent and not more than 25 per cent of the rateable value of buildings and lands as may be determined by the Corporation. This percentage may vary according to the areas and class of property. The expression 'building' includes land appurtenant to the building used for beneficial enjoyment of such building not exceeding twice the area of that building.

In addition to the rate of tax indicated above, the following cesses are also levied on the tax:

1. Health Cess	15%
2. Education Cess	10%
3. Library Cess	3%
4. Beggary Cess	3%
	31%

Thus, the final tax payable by the property owner is the property tax determined plus 31 per cent towards cesses.

Valuation of Property : The valuation of property based on the annual rental value is not easy, although it may appear simple. There are different kinds of property and the property has different values depending on the purpose for which it is used. Basically, there are two types of property—residential and non-residential. Non-residential buildings can be divided into a number of categories like shops, hotels, cinema houses, office buildings, industrial buildings and so on. In residential buildings, there are again two categories—buildings occupied by the owner or self-occupied property, and buildings which are let out or are under tenancy.

In Bangalore, the practice has been to accept the actual rent received as reasonable rent for the purpose of calculating the rental value. In the case of owner occupied property, the rent is determined on the basis of hypothetical tenancy. While calculating the gross value of a property, only the present condition of the property and the use to which it is put is taken into consideration and not what the property is likely to fetch with additions or alterations or its potential value. Sometimes, the comparison method is used, *i.e.*, rent which a particular property is said to be fetching is compared with similar properties let out in the vicinity. Wherever, rents have been determined by the competent authority under the Rent Control Act, that rent is taken as the basis for assessment.

Problems of Revision of Tax : Property taxation in Bangalore has an interesting history. According to the provisions of the City of Bangalore Municipal Corporation Act, 1949, property tax was levied at 15 per cent of the annual rateable value. In 1976, when the Karnataka Municipal Corporation Act came into force, the law itself provided for levying the tax at a minimum of 20 per cent of the annual rateable value. However, the tax actually levied was only 15 per cent of such value on residential buildings, and on non- residential buildings the rate was fixed at 20 per cent of the annual rateable value. This situation continued till September 1987.

It is worth noting here that although the proposal for enhancement of the tax from 15 to 20 per cent was made by the Corporation, the State Government turned it down in 1979 and in 1980. The reason given was that there was no elected body at that time and the proposal for enhancement would be considered after the elected body came into being. (There was no elected body in the Bangalore City Corporation for the period January 1975—August 1983). The selected body came into being in August 1983 and it took another four years for the minimum statutory rate of 20 per cent to come into effect. It was only from 1st October 1987 that the rate has been enhanced from 15 to 20 per cent on residential buildings. On non-residential buildings the rate was enhanced to 20 per cent in 1985 and to 25 per cent in 1987.

Another curious fact relates to the question of general revision of property tax. According to the Karnataka Municipal Corporation Act, it is mandatory on the part of the Corporation to revise the tax levied by it once in five years. However, no revision has taken place so far, since the year 1972. Even in 1972, the revision could not be given effect to in respect of owner-occupied residential properties. The question of general revision was taken up by the Corporation and after a great deal of discussion, it was resolved to take up general revision with effect from 1st April 1986. This decision, however, met with stiff resistance from a section of the population in the city. It was argued that taxes were high and any revision would affect the citizens adversely. The agitation generated a lot of debate on the subject and finally the State Government dropped the proposal of general revision of tax. Instead, it was decided that the rate of tax be increased by 5 per cent. The net result was that instead of a general revision which was long overdue, the property tax came to be levied on residential buildings at the statutory minimum.

Revenue from Property Tax : Although property tax continues to be the main source of revenue for the Corporation (excluding the octroi compensation grant from government), it has not proved to be much of an elastic source. The particulars of revenue derived from property tax by the Bangalore City Corporation for a period of ten years from 1977-78 are given in **Table 8.1.** While the tax demand went up by four times during this period — from Rs. 5.2 crore in 1977-78 to Rs. 20.2 crore in 1986-87, the actual collection increased by a little over three times—from Rs. 3.7 crore to Rs.11.6 crore. The percentage of collection, however, declined from 72 to 57.

TABLE 8.1 : **Revenue derived from Property Tax by Bangalore City Corporation (on buildings)**

(rupees crores)

Year	*Demand*	*Collection*	*%age of collection to demand*
1977-78	5.20	3.77	72.60
1978-79	5.72	4.02	70.32
1979-80	6.50	4.45	68.55
1980-81	7.83	5.54	70.77
1981-82	8.98	6.84	76.19
1982-83	9.83	7.53	76.59
1983-84	10.99	8.04	73.17
1984-85	12.57	8.38	66.67
1985-86	17.22	11.56	67.15
1986-87	20.21	11.66	57.68

Source : Bangalore City Corporation Annual Reports.

The rise in the quantum of tax over the years is to be attributed more to the widening of the tax net caused by addition of new areas to the Corporation and the construction of new buildings. The number of properties (built up) in Bangalore almost doubled from 1,04,905 in 1970 to 2,08,140 in 1986 (**Table 8.2**). There has thus hardly been any real effort at resource mobilisation either by way of general revision of tax or by increase in the rate of tax. Other shortcomings related to underassessment and improper assessment mainly on account of the ill-equipped implementation machinery. Valuation of properties is done by staff who are not properly trained and secondly, there is the problem of corrupt practices resulting in leakage of revenue. This phenomenon is no doubt common to all cities in India.

TABLE 8.2 : **Number of Properties in Bangalore City Corporation Area**

Year	*Buildings*	*Vacant Lands*
1970	1,04,905	16,102
1975	1,41,917	21,139
1980	1,67,604	20,257
1981	1,72,080	20,321
1982	1,79,017	21,486
1983	1,84,126	20,734
1984	1,86,774	20,694
1985	2,00,698	22,065
1986	2,08,140	19,736

Source : Bangalore City Corporation Records.

Legal Issues: The annual rental value principle is used not only in Bangalore but in a number of other cities in India, and has been subject to a great deal of litigation. The courts have interpreted the municipal law provisions relating to property tax assessment in the light of the rent control legislation and this has adversely affected this source. In substance, the Supreme Court has laid down the principle that the annual value of a building is governed by the provisions of rent control legislation and the existing 'fair rent' or 'standard rent' as defined under the Act. In the case of Deewan Doulat Roy Chaudhri *vs.* New Delhi Municipal Committee and another (AIR 1980 SC 541), the Supreme Court extended this principle further by holding that even in the case of a building in respect of which no standard rent had been fixed or where the building was self-occupied, the annual value must be limited to the measure of standard rent determinable under the Rent Control Act and the same could not be calculated on the basis of a higher rent actually received or receivable by the landlord. This has been reterated in the judgement of the Supreme Court in Dr Balbir Singh and others *vs.* MYSMCD and others. "The rateable value of a building, whether tenanted or self-occupied is limited by the measure of standard rent arrived at by the assessing authority by applying the principles laid down in the Rent Control Act and cannot exceed the figure of the standard rent so arrived at by the assessing authority.... The test, therefore, is not what is the standard rent of the building but what is the rent which the owner reasonably expects to receive from a hypothetical tenant and such reasonable expectation can in no event exceed the standard rent of the building determinable in the Rent Control Act, though it may in a given case be lower than the standard rent". (AIR 1985 SC 339).

This judicial decision has serious financial implications for the local bodies. The rents fixed under the Rent Control Act continue for years together and there would be no scope to enhance the property tax although there might be increase in the value of the property. If all buildings are to be assessed in terms of the fair rent under the Rent Control Act, the property tax would not only become inflexible but property taxation cannot serve as a useful instrument of the land policy.

It is necessary to refer to another recent court decision. The Bangalore City Corporation had assessed the building belonging to a Bank (situated on M.G. Road) at a rateable value of Rs. 3 per square foot. The assessment was challenged on the ground that:

(a) the building belonged to a bank and the bank is a part of the Central Government and cannot therefore be taxed as per the provisions of Article 285 of the Constitution, and
(b) the method of computation of the rateable value was contrary to the provisions of the Karnataka Municipal Corporation Act and was, therefore, arbitrary and unreasonable.

The High Court of Karnataka did not agree with either of these contentions and upheld the assessment made by the Bangalore City Corporation. This is significant decision for the Corporation, as otherwise all lands and buildings occupied by the banks and similar institutions or bodies which may come under the control of the government—Central or State, but nevertheless perform corporate functions, would have escaped assessment.

Tax on Vacant Land

In respect of vacant land, the Karnataka Municipal Corporation Act has not laid down any specific method of assessment. Under the Bangalore Municipal Corporation Act which was in force prior to the Karnataka Municipal Corporation Act, the Commissioner of the Corporation was authorised to determine the value of land for the purpose of assessing the property tax and accordingly, the Commissioner issued a circular to determine the same at 1/50th of the market value. Thus the annual value of a vacant land which is not let out is determined even today at 1/50th of its market value.

The particulars of vacant land tax levied and collected by the Bangalore City Corporation for ten years from 1977-78 are given in **Table 8.3.** Both demand and collection of this tax have virtually been stagnant over the years. While the demand has fluctuated between Rs. 25 and Rs. 30 lakh per annum, the collections have declined from over Rs. 17 lakh in 1978-79 to Rs. 12 lakh in 1986-87. The percentage of collection has also registered a fall from a high of 58 per cent in 1981-82 to 39 per cent in 1986-87. There has also not been any significant change in the number of vacant sites in Bangalore (**Table 8.2**). It has been hovering around 20,000 to 22,000 from 1975 onwards.

TABLE 8.3 : **Revenue derived from Vacant Land Tax by Bangalore City Corporation**

(Rupees in lakhs)

Year	*Demand*	*Collection*	*%age of collection to demand*
1977-78	27.26	12.05	44.21
1978-79	32.59	17.76	54.48
1979-80	31.44	17.53	55.74
1980-81	25.35	12.99	51.25
1981-82	28.03	16.25	57.99
1982-83	25.86	14.28	55.22
1983-84	23.67	11.60	49.01
1984-85	25.22	11.35	44.99
1985-86	28.53	14.14	49.56
1986-87	30.75	12.05	39.16

Source : Bangalore City Corporation Records.

Betterment Fee

The basic concept behind betterment levy is that increase in land values must be taxed. In Bangalore, the authority for such a levy is derived from the provisions of Section 18 of the Karnataka Town and Country Planning Act. According to this provision, the Planning Authority may levy a fee, whenever, it grants permission for a change in the use or development of any land or building and such change or development is capable of yielding a better income to the owner. The fee levied should not exceed one-third of the estimated increase in the value of the land or building. The Karnataka Planning Authority Rules prescribe the fees for grant of such permission.

The betterment fees for different uses were fixed in 1976 and revised after a gap of ten years in 1986. The rates prescribed under the Rules and the revenue derived from this levy are given in **Table 8.4**. The levy in respect of commercial use is the highest (Rs. 25 per sq.metre), followed by industrial use (Rs. 10 per sq.metre), and residential use (Rs. 5 per sq.metre). The revision of rates in 1986 by over two times is reflected in the revenues for the years 1986-87—Rs. 12.13 lakh, an increase of 320 per cent over the previous year (Rs. 2.8 lakh). The year 1987-88 has also shown a significant rise of 46 per cent (Rs. 17.55 lakh) compared to the preceding year.

TABLE 8.4 : **Betterment Fee for Different Land Uses in Bangalore**

Use	*Fee (per sq. metre)*	
	1976 Rs.	*1986 Rs.*
Residential	2.00	5.00
Industrial	5.00	10.00
Commercial	10.00	25.00

Revenue from Betterment Fee

(Rupees in lakhs)

Year	*Revenue realised*	*Percentage increase*
1985-86	2.88	—
1986-87	12.13	319.9
1087-88	17.75	46.33

Source : Bangalore Development Authority and Bangalore City Corporation Records.

Betterment fee is levied under the Karnataka Town and Country Planning Act under two circumstances :

(a) when a person wants to change the use of land or building,

(b) when development takes place on a land or building—in either case, it must be capable of yielding better income to the owner.

The issue of betterment levy is also related to the system of planning permissions under the Karnataka Town and Country Planning Act. According to Section 14 of the Act, once a development plan has been approved, every change in land use and every development will have to conform to the provisions of the plan and no change in land use or development can be made without the written permission of the Planning Authority. While the term 'change in land use' is easily understandable, the expression 'development' has given rise to technical and operational problems. According to the Explanation under Section 14 of the Karnataka Town and Country Planning Act, the expression 'development' means "the carrying out of the building or other operation in or over or under any land or the making of any material change in the use of any building or other land." Certain operations or uses of land are not deemed to involve development, such as maintenance, improvement or alteration works of a building which affect only the interior of the building, carrying out of works in compliance with the directions given by any legal authority, uses within the curtilage of a dwelling house for any purpose incidental to the enjoyment of dwelling use, etc. Strictly speaking, 'development' would cover any new construction or major alterations to an existing building or the improvement of a piece of vacant land for the purposes of even carrying on sports activities. Again, when an existing building is to be developed or when a new structure is put up in the compound of an existing building, how much area is to be taken into account for calculating the betterment fee—the entire sital area or the floor area or the plinth area of the building, is not clear. The Rule merely states that the fee is to be levied per sq.mt. of land. Thus 'development' as defined in the Karnataka Town and Country Planning Act for the purpose of levying the betterment fee is vague and ambiguous.

STAMP DUTY AND REGISTRATION CHARGES

When immovable property is transferred in the Bangalore Metropolitan Area two kinds of levies are attracted—stamp duty and registration charges.

Under the Registration Act, 1908, certain documents relating to transfer of immoveable property will have to be compulsorily registered.

Such documents may be instruments of gifts of immoveable property or non-testamentary instruments which create, limit or extinguish any right, title or interest of the value exceeding Rs. 100 in immoveable properties or leases of immoveable property for any term exceeding one year. Registration charges are levied for the registration of all such documents. The charges are levied on an *ad valorem* scale on the amount or value of the property. The *ad valorem* scale prescribed by government ranges from Rs. 0.75 when the amount or value does not exceed Rs. 50 to Rs. 10 for every Rs. 1,000 or part thereof in excess of Rs. 5,000.

Stamp duty is payable under Karnataka Stamp Act, 1957 on certain instruments relating to conveyance of transfer or immoveable property. The stamp duty payable for different types of conveyances are prescribed in the Schedule to the Act. The duty ranges from Rs. 5 where the market value of the property does not exceed Rs. 50 to Rs. 100, where the value exceeds Rs. 900 plus Rs. 50 for every Rs. 500 or part thereof in excess of Rs. 1,000. The State derives fairly substantial revenue from stamp duty and registration charges. However, since these fees are levied on different types of transactions, which include moveable property, it has not been possible to know the exact revenue from the transactions relating to immoveable properties. It may, however, be noted that the revenue from these two levies for Bangalore District was of the order of Rs. 27.8 crore during 1987-88. The major portion of the revenue accrues from immovable property.

TAXATION AS INSTRUMENT OF LAND POLICY

A review of the various fiscal measures relating to land and property is called for in the light of the recent trends in urban development and socio-economic growth, so that taxation can serve as an effective instrument of Urban Land Policy.

Property Tax continues to occupy a central place in the system of local taxation in India despite the fact that it has not proved to be a very buoyant source of revenue. A number of Committees have gone into the question of property tax reform — the Local Finance Enquiry Committee (1951), the Taxation Enquiry Committee (1955), the Committee on Augmentation of Financial Resources for Urban Local Bodies, otherwise known as Zakaria Committee (1963), the Rural-Urban Relationship Committee (1966), all set up by the Government of India, and the Mysore Taxation and Resources Enquiry Committee (1969), the Taxation Review

Committee (1981) and the Local Finance Commission (1985) set up by the Government of Karnataka. The curious aspect of these reports is that "apart from a few exceptions, they have reached the same conclusions and made similar recommendations over a span of almost twenty years; yet few of their major recommendations have been put into practice" (Rakesh Mohan, 1983). The NCEAR Study (1980) which surveyed 51 Municipal bodies in India identified the following main problems with regard to property tax :

(a) uniform methods of property valuation have not been evolved;
(b) in the absence of the above, local influences affect the valuation in all kinds of ways;
(c) inadequate manpower-quantity as well as quality;
(d) there are intrinsic conflicts between the provisions of the Rent Control Acts and the assessment of rateable value for Property tax. Reassessment of properties is also affected by the operation of Rent Control Acts; and
(e) lack of enforcement machinery to enforce timely payments.

The reforms suggested in the field of property taxation are the following:

(a) assessment of property tax on the basis of capital value instead of annual rateable value;
(b) Site Value taxation;
(c) determination of a basic tax related to the plinth area and surcharge on excess appurtenant land which is greater than three times the built up area; and
(d) composite area—linked system—delinked from the rental value system.

The systems at (a) and (b) above have been discussed at the beginning of this chapter. The proposal at (c) envisages a basic tax on the basis of the plinth area (Ramakrishna, 1980). For buildings with appurtenant land which exceeds three times the built up area, there will be a surcharge. Extra charges would be levied according to location, type of construction, the nature of its use and the age of the building. Each of these variables will have five or six categories and every building will be classified into one of these. The advantages claimed for this system are that owners can pay on a self-assessment basis once the parameters of the scheme are worked out, the scope for discretion on the part of valuation officers would be reduced, the effort and expense in revision of the tax would be saved, variation of taxes can be made by altering basic rates and progressivity in taxation can be achieved by fixing the extras in a manner that would benefit the poor.

The composite area-linked system proposed at (d) above (Kapoor, 1977) is based on the following conceptual framework :

(i) Property tax would be delinked from the rent based rateable value concept;

(ii) The occupier, whether owner or tenant, would be liable to pay the tax; and

(iii) Properties would be classified into homogenous zones and assessment would be based on certain criteria like use to which a premises is put, age of the building and type of construction. This system is somewhat similar to the area based system at (c) and similar advantages are claimed. Basically, these new concepts have tried to move away from the system based on annual rental value and lay down certain criteria for valuation. The assumption is that 'variables' used are easily measurable. In practice, however, it would be difficult to measure all the influences which go to determine property values.

Reform of property tax is a complex issue involving legal and administrative problems. Nevertheless, it is imperative in view of its importance not only as source of revenue to the local bodies but as an instrument of land policy. While it may not be possible to find a foolproof method of assessment, any future reform must be based on the premise of delinking property tax from rent control. The following reforms are suggested in respect of Bangalore.

(a) The annual rental value system may be replaced by capital valuation basis. This would help in capturing the increasing land values for public benefit. Secondly, it would free property tax from the clutches of rent control law. Moreover, in a developing country it is normally more advantageous to use a capital value base (Ursula Hicks, 1967). Other advantages of capital value taxation are that it makes a more correct estimate of economic importance and, therefore, the taxable capacity of the owner (Gyanchand, 1947), it would lead to better collection of taxes as some of the Central taxes are based on capital valuation and as such it would be more difficult to evade taxation, and finally the developmental or potential value of the property is reflected in the assessment which is based on the market selling price.

(b) Capital valuation should also take into account factors like the use characteristics and location of the building. A set of guidelines must be evolved to assist the valuation officers in arriving at the correct value.

(c) A Central Valuation Agency consisting of qualified persons must be set up for Bangalore to carry out the assessment of properties. This will reduce arbitrariness and impart greater objectivity in the valuation process.

(d) The rate of tax should be fixed such that the house building activity particularly for the weaker sections is encouraged. This is important to achieve the policy objective of providing adequate housing to the growing population.

As a tool of Land Use Planning, taxation of vacant land in urban and urbanisable areas can play a vital role. This has been tried in some countries. In Spain, a special tax is levied on vacant land declared as urbanised. The rates are as follows :

Soon after declaration as urbanised area	0.5 per cent of market value or expected value after development
After provision of infrastructure	Two per cent of market value
After 5 years, if site unused for construction purpose	Five per cent of market value

In Chile, tax on vacant sites takes effect five years after a detailed planning scheme has been approved. The rate is one per cent of the assessed value to begin with and goes on increasing by one per cent each year up to six per cent until the land is put to use for the purpose of construction.

Syria has a differential rate of tax on vacant land. The rate increases with increase in site value :

Site Value (US $)	*Tax Rate*
Less than 12,050	1%
12,051 to 24,100	2%
24,101 to 73,100	3%
73,101 to 1,24,500	4%
1,24,500 and above	5%

Those keeping the land vacant for speculative purposes will pay more under this system. Similarly, in Taiwan there is a progressive rate of tax on vacant land of two to five times the basic property tax rate, with exception to small land owners desiring to construct their own dwelling.

There is great scope to employ vacant land tax as an instrument of land policy as also to augment revenues in an expanding city like Bangalore. It can be used to control speculation and to increase the pace of housing/construction activity in developed areas. The rate of tax now levied by the Corporation on vacant land is ridiculously low and only helps to promote speculation. There are several vacant sites in the areas developed by the Bangalore Development Authority. Although there is provision in the rules to resume land that has not been put to use for which it has been allotted within a period of three years, this has not been resorted to so far. With no disincentive to keep the land vacant, speculators thrive. In view of certain practical problems in resuming the land not utilised within the specified period, the best course seems to be to levy a progressive rate of tax—the rate increasing every year, which would act as a spur to development on the one hand and as a source of revenue on the other.

Darin-Drabkin (1977), has suggested that taxation which reduces the demand for land and increases the supply to the market may be evaluated as an efficient land taxation system. While generally a high rate of tax will increase the price of a good, a heavy tax on land may lead to a lower level of land prices. Unlike other goods, land cannot be produced and has no cost of production (except the costs of infrastructure). Land derives its value from the revenue expected from it in the present or in the future. A high rate of tax on vacant land increases the cost of capital investment in land property and diminishes the attractiveness of land as a source of capital investment. The reduced demand for land as a capital investment and the high maintenance costs of vacant land may result in lower prices and increased supply of land to the market. In the case of built land, however, high maintenance cost may not have the same effect where the demand for housing and commercial buildings is high. Here, a higher level of taxation may lead to a higher price for such buildings.

Instead of redistribution of wealth, this may affect the citizens adversely. However, if the tax level remains high and the demand for real estate gets reduced in the long run, investment in real estate may also become less attractive.

Shortage of land in desirable locations leads to a higher price level. Higher tax levels in such areas may not influence the price of land but may reduce or eliminate the level of profit from land and influence the redistribution of wealth. Part of the additional value created by the urbanisation process by the few land owners can be used to cover the costs of urban investments.

It is suggested that a separate legislation be enacted in respect of property tax including tax on urban and urbanisable vacant land in Bangalore.

The policy on levy of a tax on betterment or development needs to be clearly defined. As of now, this levy is viewed mostly from the angle of increasing revenue. It has not consciously been used as an instrument of land policy. Considerations of efficiency and equity have not been given due importance. Betterment levies can be used to introduce discipline into the demand for public expenditure. The expenditure on development specific to the site or a layout can be met from the betterment levy instead of from the general revenues. The levy can serve as an effective means to finance public investment. Where it is not possible to provide public services on a cost recovery basis, the taxation of land value can be used to finance the services.

The betterment fees now fixed are uniform (for a particular land use) throughout Bangalore Metropolitan Area. A piece of land in the Central Business District or in the core area of a city has a higher potential in terms of gain or income than the same extent of land in the periphery. It would be prudent to levy higher rates in the central areas compared to the areas away from the city centre. The rates can vary depending on the locational advantage of the sites. A progressive tax rate depending on the extent or area to be developed—a higher rate can be levied for larger areas—can be introduced. This can also help to achieve the objective of equity.

It is not easy to devise a satisfactory tax system relating to land. It is 'virtually impossible to devise a tax that will directly reduce in substantial degree, or directly capture a significant part of the increment in the value of land resulting from this conversion to urban use. Almost any kind of tax will mostly be passed on the final consumer of the developed land' (Neutze, 1970). Nevertheless, the above measures can help in moving nearer the goals of land policy.

9

SUMMARY AND CONCLUSIONS

This chapter presents a summary of the major findings of the study and discusses the vital issues arising from the study and the possible opportunities for the future.

SUMMARY OF FINDINGS

Policy Perspectives

The rapid growth in population and the process of urbanisation have resulted in an increasing demand for urban land. The shortage of land has given rise to problems relating to shelter, land use, legal rights over the land and rising land prices. These problems have necessitated State intervention in the urban land market. Hence the need for an Urban Land Policy. Urban land problems are complex and the Urban Land Use Pattern is the result of a variety of operative forces. As such, the formulation of Urban Land Policy is a difficult task. While the conceptual basis for such a policy may be found in the theories relating to urban land use, urban land values and Urban Land Use Planning, the formulation of a coherent policy depends on a number of factors peculiar to each country or region.

Although no Urban Land Policy has been formulated as such in India, statements reflecting the State policy can be gathered from the following sources: (i) Reports of various committees of the government; (ii) Five Year Plans; and (iii) the relevant legislations. The important reports and documents which have dealt with Urban Land Policy are the Committee on Urban Land Policy (1965), the Task Force on Housing and Urban Development (1983), the National Commission on Urbanisation (1988) and the National Housing Policy Statement (1988).

The stated objectives of Urban Land Policy in India are:

(a) to achieve an optimum social use of urban land;
(b) to make land available in adequate quantity at the right time and for reasonable prices;
(c) to encourage co-operative and individual effort in land development, housing and construction;
(d) to widen the base of land ownership and to safeguard the interests of the poor;
(e) to encourage the socially and economically efficient allocation of urban land; and
(f) to promote flexibility in land-use in response to changes resulting from a growing city.

The instruments used for implementation of the above objectives are :

(i) Legal and regulatory measures—Master Plan including land use control measures like zoning, building regulations and sub-division regulations;
(ii) Fiscal measures consisting of various forms of taxes and levies notably property tax;
(iii) Development measures like programmes of land acquisition and development; and
(iv) Urban land ceiling to achieve equitable distribution of land and to prevent speculation.

None of the above-stated objectives has been achieved in India. Although a considerable quantity of land has been acquired and distributed, the demand has outpaced the supply. A major failure is in controlling the rising land values. Land in the open market has become too costly to be afforded by the common man. Urban Land Policy measures have, by and large, favoured the rich at the cost of the poor.

Bangalore—The Study Area

Bangalore has witnessed remarkable growth in size and population since the beginning of this century. The area of Bangalore City increased from 28.85 sq.kms in 1901 to 151 sq.kms in 1981 (five times). The area of Urban Agglomeration in 1981 was 365.65 sq.kms and that of the Metropolitan Area was 500 sq.kms.

Bangalore has a poor rural hinterland. The urban growth of the area within a radius of 70 km (zone of influence) has an important bearing on the spatial planning of Bangalore from a regional perspective.

The population of Bangalore increased from 0.23 million in 1901 to 2.39 million in 1981 (13 times). The decade 1971-81 recorded a growth rate of 76 per cent, the highest for any metropolitan city in India. During the period of 1951-81, it was observed that the peripheral area registered a higher growth rate compared to the City Corporation area and the Metropolitan area as a whole.

Migrants constitute about 37 per cent of the population in Bangalore. Majority of them come from the four southern states. The largest number of people, however, migrate from within the State of Karnataka itself. The migrants from urban areas (58 per cent) is more than from rural area (42 per cent). The largest number of people migrate for the purpose of employment (30 per cent), followed by the family being moved (29 per cent), marriage (18 per cent) and education (6 per cent).

The density of Bangalore city went up from 13 per acre in 1911 to 46 per cent per acre in 1981, the intracity variations in density have ranged from less than 30 to over 300 per acre. The pattern of population distribution has shown bi-nodality—one centering around City market and the other near Russel market. By and large, Bangalore has remained a low density city, except near the city nuclei.

The occupational structure of Bangalore shows that 30 per cent of the population constituted the work force in 1981 and of them, 37 per cent were engaged in manufacturing, 18.5 per cent in trade and commerce, 9 per cent in transport, storage and communication and about 26 per cent in other services with agriculture claiming only 2.8 per cent of the population.

Bangalore enjoys regional primacy, accounting for 7.8 per cent of Karnataka's population and 26 per cent of the urban population of the State. The tremendous growth of Bangalore accompanied by socio-economic development has resulted in shortages in infrastructure and civic amenities and the problem of urban land has become critical. Hence, the need to formulate an appropriate land policy for the Bangalore Metropolitan Area.

Urban Land Values

The urban land values are influenced by macro economic factors like rapid urbanisation, population growth, etc., and the peculiar factors influencing the Urban Land Market like location, accessibility, change of land use and Land Use Controls. The combined effect of these factors has been an increase in land values in cities.

An analysis of changes in land values in Bangalore in time and space reveals the following :

The average land values in Bangalore based on the registered values showed an increase of about 300 per cent between 1975-76 and 1986-87. For certain localities, the increase varied between 100-1200 per cent. With reference to base years 1950-51, 1960- 61 and 1970-71, the percentage increase in the price levels was 4,215, 2,159 and 1,257 respectively. The localities in the central part of the city and those with high socio-economic status showed a higher rate of increase, while the peripheral and low status localities showed relatively lower rate of increase.

The price at which the BDA has sold the sites to public has been revised thrice since 1975 and has risen five to six times in a period of 12 years. The price fetched by BDA in the auctions has ranged from Rs. 110 to Rs. 200 per sq.ft during the last five years.

The values fixed by State Government in 1975 were revised in 1982 and 1985. But the notification issued by the Government in this regard has been quashed by the High Court of Karnataka.

The data collected informally from the Real Estate Agents reveals that the value of land in Bangalore increased by 20 times between 1983 and 1987 and by 10 times between 1980 and 1987. Compared to the registration prices, the values gathered from Estate Agents shows a variation ranging from 20 per cent to 150 per cent.

The spatial distribution of land values shows that the values in the central parts of the cities are higher compared to other areas. There is a declining pattern of land values with distance from the city centre, although the rate of increase has been higher in the newly developed extensions of BDA. Land in commercial areas are found to have higher values than in the residential areas. The low price level in the rural-urban fringe has promoted speculation. The high land value and low rental value in CBD has resulted in deterioration of the old building stock.

No credible record of land prices is available in Bangalore. The registration prices shows a gross under-valuation of land in order to evade registration fees. The allotment price of BDA is kept low to subsidise the weaker sections and the auction rates reflect an element of scarcity value as land is released to the market in small pieces.

The major factors contributing to increase in the land values in Bangalore are the rapid growth of population, inflationary trends, speculation, changing social trends and the inability of BDA to provide adequate land to the public at the desired pace. The efforts of government in controlling land price through public acquisition of land, by restricting ownership rights and through other measures under the Urban Land Ceiling Law have failed. A hypothesis can be postulated that where the disparity between the price of land in the market and that offered by a public authority is very wide and the quantity of land supplied by the public authority is small, the market price will continue to be high.

Land Use Planning in Bangalore

Two Master Plans have been prepared for Bangalore Metropolitan Area —The Outline Development Plan (1972) and the Comprehensive Development Plan (1984). The two plans examined the existing land uses and proposed increases in the area under different uses on the basis of population requirement at the end of the plan period.

The changes in the land use pattern during the two decade period 1961-83 reveal that the total area under different land uses in Bangalore increased by 7,120 acres between 1961 and 1972 and by 15,585 acres between 1972 and 1983. Between 1961 and 1983, the developed area of the city increased by 22,100 acres (80 %). The defence authorities still occupy a considerable extent of land in the city (5,222) acres. The actual utilisation of land fell short of what was planned in ODP. The shortfall was particularly marked in respect of industrial use (35 %).

The vast planning area of 1,279 sq.km. provided under CDP, though aimed at meeting the requirements of a population of 7 million by 2001 and providing an adequate green belt is bound to promote extensive development of the city. The policy of BDA of acquiring vast stretches of land in the periphery has contributed to expansion of the urban sprawl.

The vacant lands between developed areas and unplanned developments in the periphery have resulted in uneconomic utilisation of land.

The land use proposed in CDP based on railway alignments is dependent on mass transportation system prevalent in Western cities. This is a costly process and is fraught with serious implementation problems.

Although the two development plans provided for a vast vacant area to serve as green belt (235 sq.km in ODP and 840 sq.km in CDP), large scale inroads have been made into the green belt. The preservation of green belt has proved to be extremely difficult in view of the growing demand for urban land in Bangalore, mainly for housing. It is, therefore, necessary to adopt a more pragmatic policy on green belt with reference to its purpose, size and pattern.

Land Use Control is exercised through zoning regulations, building byelaws and subdivision regulations. The development in Bangalore has traditionally been more extensive than intensive, though high rise buildings, especially for commercial purposes are now permitted in certain areas. There have been a number of deviations from the zonal planning. Land use changes have taken place both with and without legal permission. Agricultural land is converted for non-agricultural purposes in the periphery without reference to the Planning Authority and residential land is being changed to commercial use in the city unauthorisedly. Buildings have been constructed in violation of building byelaws. The building byelaws, however, need to be amended with a view to free the builders from rigid controls.

Industrial development has contributed a great deal to the sprawl of Bangalore city. However, no specific policy seems to have guided the location of industries in an around the city. Initially, the easy and cheap availability of land facilitated location of industries in all directions of the city. In spite of the policy of government to avoid further concentration of industries in and around Bangalore and to disperse them to industrially backward areas, the city continues to be the most attractive place for entrepreneurs in view of the facilities it offers and also on account of dilution of the policy. Industrial development in Bangalore (like in many other places in the country) has taken place without any relation to the Urban Planning Process. It is, therefore, necessary to integrate the policies relating to urban development and industrial development.

There is need for a departure from the existing narrow approach of identifying Land Use Plan with zoning and land use restrictions. It should be related to the city functions and other needs of the people like housing and employment.

Land Acquisition and Disposal

In Bangalore, land is acquired by public authorities through different legislations. The methods of acquisition are: compulsory acquisition under the Land Acquisition Act, acquisition through negotiation and acquisition of surplus land under the Urban Land Ceiling Act.

There is enormous delay in the process of acquisition. The BDA could acquire only 9,580 acres out of 18,643 acres notified for acquisition between 1976 and 1988. The average time taken by BDA to complete the acquisition proceedings is 4.5 years, although in some cases it has taken nearly ten years. The acquisition of land by Karnataka Industrial Area Development Board for industrial purposes has been, by and large, speedy. The Board has acquired land through negotiations with land owners in a number of cases.

The problems faced in the process of acquisition mainly pertain to procedural aspects, valuation of property and determination of compensation and litigation. The compensation determined by the Land Acquisition Officer is invariably enhanced by the Courts. Thus, the acquiring bodies end up spending huge amounts, long after the acquisition is over.

Land has been acquired by the State Government for a number of House Building Co-operative Societies. The Societies also acquire land through direct purchase from the land owners. While the co-operative sector has helped in adding to the housing stock of Bangalore, it has also contributed to the haphazard development in the fringe areas of the city.

Under the Urban Land Ceiling Act, 3,443 acres of land have been acquired since the law came into force in 1976. This is just four per cent of the area declared as excess by land owners. A large number of exemptions have been granted under the Act. The surplus land acquired is located mostly in the periphery. The main objectives of the law, *viz.*, to control speculation and the rising land values and ensure equitable distribution by making available sufficient land for weaker sections have not been achieved.

In view of its almost total failure, it is suggested that the Urban Land Ceiling and Regulation Act be deleted from the statute book. NCU's suggestion relating to providing moratorium of five years to the land owner for development of the vacant lands according to certain prescribed norms is, however, not likely to serve the aims of the law any further than hitherto. Even now, where exemptions are granted by the Government, conditions regarding development or utilisation of the land within a specified period are imposed. In practice, these conditions are hardly enforced. Moreover, a Five year moratorium is too long a period, considering the fact that over 15 years have already passed since the coming into force of the Act and the process of taking over the surplus land should have been completed long back. In a city like Bangalore, a considerable part of the surplus land has already been granted exemptions. The operation of the law is fraught with serious administrative difficulties. The only way out seems to be to adopt a radical measure of declaring all the remaining surplus land as having vested in the State Government with immediate effect. A more practical method would be to involve the land owners in achieving the spirit of the law. Schemes can be formulated to provide for the proper utilisation of the land. Housing is not the only use to which the surplus land could be put (as NCU seems to assume). Lot of land particularly in the pheripery is under agricultural or horticultural use. It would be wise to encourage land uses which add to the greenery and add to agricultural/horticultural produce.

There is no clear policy guiding distribution of land. As per the Rules of the BDA, 30 per cent of the sites in a layout is reserved for persons belonging to economically weaker sections at 50 per cent of the value of the site. Sites are also reserved for different categories like scheduled castes, scheduled tribes, persons of armed forces, government employees etc. Commercial sites and residential sites which are corner sites are sold through public auction.

The performance of BDA in land distribution leaves much to be desired. Totally, 41,921 sites were distributed between 1976 and 1986-87, averaging about 3,000 sites a year. This is far short of the requirements of a fast growing city like Bangalore.

The efforts of government in providing access to land to the poor in Bangalore are not adequate. Continuation of the policy of public subsidy is inescapable to improve accessibility of land and shelter to the poor. There is also a need for shift in bias towards the weaker sections. It is suggested that 50 per cent of the sites formed by BDA be allocated to the poor and low income categories.

It is necessary to evolve new policies which will help in quicker acquisition of land and speedy delivery. Innovative techniques like land pooling, excess acquisition and guided development need to be tried. Scrapping of the Urban Land Ceiling Act may help in quicker releases of land in the land market and exercise a healthy influence on rising land prices. There is need for coordination between land acquisition and land use polices.

Fiscal Policies

The various types of taxes levied in respect of urban land in Bangalore are : Property tax, vacant land tax, Betterment fee and Stamp duty and Registration charges.

Property tax is based on the annual rental value of the property. Although there is an increase in the quantum of revenue derived by the Corporation over the years (from Rs. 3.7 crore in 1977-78 to Rs. 11.6 crore in 1986-87), the percentage of collection has shown a declining trend (from 72 to 57 during the same period). It has not been possible to take up revision of property tax in Bangalore since 1972, although it is mandatory to do so once in five years. The Rent Control Law and Judicial Decisions have acted as inhibiting factors in the true valuation of property. Suggested reforms include replacement of Annual Rental Value System by capital valuation system which will also take into account use characteristics and location of building, setting up a Central Valuation Agency and a rate structure that promotes low cost house building activity.

The tax on vacant land is very low - 1/50th of the market value of the land. This has remained a static source of income. The revenue actually declined from Rs. 17 lakh in 1978-79 to Rs. 12 lakh in 1986-87. There is a great scope to employ the vacant land tax as an instrument of land policy - both to increase the income and control speculation. Enactment of a separate legislation in this regard including property tax is suggested.

There has been a significant rise of revenue through betterment levy after the revision of rates in 1986—from Rs. 2.8 lakh in 1985-86, it shot up to over Rs. 12 lakh in 1986-87. It is also possible to use the betterment levy as an instrument of land policy, especially as a means to finance investment and services. The rate structure needs to be revised to make it more progressive in place of the uniform structure now prevailing.

ISSUES ARISING OUT OF THE STUDY

At the conclusion of the study, it is worthwhile reflecting on the critical issues in the field of Urban Land Policy and the possible approaches for the future. The major issues that arise are as follows:

Conflict between Short-term Needs and Long-term Goals

No where is man's struggle for existence reflected more clearly than in the struggle for land. Limited in quantity, land is required to satisfy a multitude of needs. Growing population, rising incomes and a number of socio-economic factors have intensified the competition for land. In urban areas, land problems are becoming more and more complex because of the interaction between land uses, land prices, land rights and land requirements for private and public purposes.

The rapid growth of metropolitan cities like Bangalore has led to paradoxical situations. Industrialisation and economic growth have generated employment and higher incomes. The supply of goods and services has increased. But there is shortage of decent housing, there is congestion in the central and old localities, middle class residents are moving to outlying extensions, the steep increase in the number of vehicles without corresponding improvement in the road network has led to traffic congestion, there are more highrise buildings and less of green and open space, there is growing prosperity but no signs of urban poverty being wiped out. Migrants continue to pour into large cities in search of jobs. There is an urgent need to improve civic amenities and infrastructural facilities but adequate resources are not forthcoming.

The use of land is affected by these contradictions in the urban scene. There are conflicts between the short-term needs of the population (like housing) and long-term planning for the city. Individual private needs may be at variance with the interests of the public at large. Acquiring a piece of land may be necessary for forming a road which is in public interest but may be the only source of livelihood to the individual. Technological progress has created new needs demanding more land; it has also made possible new ways of using land. Socio-economic changes also influence the land use patterns of a city. The increasing role of the State has created a need for more space for public buildings. In Bangalore, captains of the corporate sector are vying with one another to gain access to valuable urban space. Market forces operate to the advantage of the rich and powerful groups. The State is unable to counter these forces with the required speed and efficiency. "The difficulties in Land Use Planning result from the contradiction between the rapid technological changes which influence urban growth and the slow process of planning which allocates land use." (Darin-Drabkin, 1977).

Reconciling the competing claims of urban society and resolving the conflict between immediate requirements and long term plans is a critical issue facing urban policy makers.

Identification of Appropriate Objectives

An important finding of this work is that none of the stated objectives of Urban Land Policy has been achieved. At least part of the reason for this failure can be attributed to the type of objectives formulated and their lack of clarity.

Expressions like "optimum social use of urban land", "widening the base of land ownership", "preventing the concentraration of ownership in a few hands" represent more the articulation of a philosophy than specific objectives capable of easy realisation. Indeed, these very objectives have gone completely awry and the ground reality seems to make a mockery of them. With urban land prices ruling so high, land use is determined more by the land developers and real estate agents. The urban land market reflects the negation of the principles of equitable distribution and optimum social use. Public authorities like BDA, under compulsion to generate sufficient funds to carry on their activities are not able to make a dent on the market. Even objectives like making land available 'in adequate quantity', 'at the right time' and 'for reasonable price' are rather vague and need to be defined more precisely in the Indian context of wide economic and social disparities.

In formulating Urban Land Policy, therefore, it is important to define objectives which are clear and implementable in the Indian or regional situation.

Strategies for Implementation

The main strategy conventionally employed to achieve the objectives of Urban Land Policy is the Master Plan. As already noted, such planning consists largely of Land Use Planning as an aid to development control. Two problems arise in adopting this approach. First, the manner of land use allocation and the standards of development do not match the socio-economic needs of the city. Zoning ignores certain realities of the Indian situation — like where people live, where they work, what they do and what their economic levels are? For instance, it is estimated that 45 to 50 per cent of employment in urban India is provided by the informal sector. This implies that nearly half of the work sites will be spread out across the city rather than being concentrated in specific zones. Much of the informal business in a city is conducted on a small scale and often operated from the premises where the entrepreneurs live—such a development is in evidence in Bangalore. But the Master Plan would drive all small scale firms to designated locations. Thus there is no correlation between employment structure and land use.

Secondly, the investment implications of a Master Plan do not match the availability of resources. For instance, the CDP of Bangalore has estimated the cost of developments proposed (like land acquisition, formation of roads, housing etc.) at Rs. 550 crore. The Plan assumes that the cost will be met out of resources from different sources—grants from government, loans from financial institutions, internal generation and also by private investment. But there is no detailed exercise of matching resources and investment, with the result implementation suffers.

Effective implementation of the Plan depends to a large extent on institutional capabilities. Public authorities like BDA and DDA have functioned more as real estate agencies—buying, developing and selling land. Planning considerations reflecting the larger interests of city development and the needs of the majority of the people, especially the weaker sections have not received adequate attention. The operation of a number of authorities in a metropolitan area—the City Corporation, the BDA, the Slum Clearance Board, the Industrial Area Development Board, etc., as in the case of Bangalore—has resulted in lack of coordination between planning and development activities.

Legal Framework

A serious problem in the field of urban management is the use of variegated legal tools. The multiplicity of laws concerning town planning, land ceiling, land acquisition and development control have resulted in confusion to the common man and has placed a strain on the law enforcement authorities. There are inconsistencies in legal provisions and conflicts in jurisdiction. For instance, conversion of agricultural land for urban uses requires permission from the Deputy Commissioner under the Land Revenue Act. At the same time, change of land use in the metropolitan area needs approval from the Planning Authority under the Town and Country Planning Act. There are as many as five acts in Karnataka containing provisions relating to land acquisition and some of them have prescribed procedures for acquisition different from those under the original Land Acquisition Act.

Compliance with various legal provisions often results in delay in implementation of programmes. The procedures to be followed, as under the Land Acquisition Act, are lengthy and cumbersome. Sometimes different authorities have to be approached for clearance as in the case of building permission. Another consequence of the numerous laws is the enormous amount of litigation. This eventually results in hardship to the citizens, especially the poorer sections who cannot afford to meet the legal costs. The wealthy exploit the legal loopholes to their own benefit as in the case of the Urban Land Ceiling Act.

There is an urgent need for a review of all the existing legislation pertaining to land and urban planning with a view to simplifying and rationalising them.

Land Information System

One difficulty while dealing with urban matters in general and land issues in particular is the absence of proper urban land records. It is interesting to note that the land record system in rural India is far more reliable and efficient than in urban India. Throughout this study, a serious handicap experienced was to obtain accurate data—whether it pertained to land use, land prices, land acquisition or details of ownership of land.

Even where data is available (*e.g.* records relating to property tax), access to data is extremely difficult. There is no single department or agency in Bangalore maintaining all the required particulars relating to land in up-to-date form. The department of Survey and Settlement undertook a city survey in the year 1965. The city has expanded considerably since then. As there are a number of authorities dealing with land, a researcher or even an administrator or a policy maker has to approach all these organisations to gain a proper and a full picture of the land scene of the Bangalore Metropolitan Region. The Bangalore City Corporation maintains records of the property owners in its jurisdiction—both in respect of vacant sites and built up property. The transfer of ownership is also recorded as and when they are reported. However, it does not have an up-to-date record of its own property, *i.e.*, land belonging to the Corporation, which could be either in its possession or leased out for some purpose. There is no monitoring of utilisation of the land leased. Sometimes, the use for which the land was leased would have been changed; at times the land would have been sub-leased. There is also no proper check over the encroachment of the Corporation property.

In the area beyond the jurisdiction of the Corporation, but within the metropolitan area, the BDA, HAL Sanitary Board, ITI Notified Area and the municipalities concerned maintain their own land records. Agricultural land or land known as 'revenue land' comes under the purview of the Revenue Department. Hence all the records pertaining to conversion of agricultural land would be with the Revenue Department, but those concerning land use under the Master Plan would be with the BDA. There is no system of reporting changes permitted by the Revenue Department to BDA.

So far as land prices are concerned, there is no public authority maintaining a correct record. One has to approach the Registration authorities to ascertain the registered prices or the BDA to know the prices of allotment or auction. While the registered prices do not reflect the true value of land, the BDA price does not represent the market value either.

The Task Force on Housing and Urban Development (Government of India, 1983) stressed the need for an improved system of land records in terms of prices as well as owners and suggested the preparation of comprehensive register of all land owners in cities and a Land Price System to provide a reliable pricing guide which included publication of land prices every year. The NCU has also emphasised the importance of building up a comprehensive data base on urban land. It has suggested the establishment of a Settlement Survey of India at the national level to make scientific surveys of land in an urban context and a Directorate of Urban Land in each State which would prepare land records in all urban centres. It has also suggested the appointment of Urban Land Manager under the Collector or designation of the Commissioner of the City Corporation as Land Manager. For Karnataka, a separate Directorate of Urban Land does not appear to be necessary. What is required is strengthening of the City Survey wing in the existing Directorate of Land Records so that the surveys are completed in time and the records are updated periodically. The suggestion of designating the Commissioner of the Corporation as Land Manager or appointing a separate officer under the collector cannot also solve the problem so far as Bangalore city is concerned, or any other metropolitan city for that matter. The respective authorities vested with necessary powers under the law have to deal with the land transactions in various forms under their jurisdiction. What is required is a system of maintenance of the records by each authority in a proper and complete manner. There could be a land records manager in each of these organisations like the Corporation, BDA etc. The BMRDA can maintain a master copy of all the lands falling under its jurisdiction. There could be a Director of Land Information in the BMRDA responsible for maintaining the land information system for the entire metropolitan region of Bangalore.

PROSPECTS —NEED FOR INTEGRATED URBAN LAND POLICY

The land factor—its use, non-use and misuse—exercises a profound influence on the process of socio-economic development in general and on the pattern of urban development in particular. If "behind much of the urban chaos lies the total mismanagement of land as the principal resource for urbanisation" (NCU, 1988), the proper management of land holds the key to orderly development.

In the first place, land must be treated as a resource. Urban land is a scarce resource whose management has to be planned with utmost care. The concept of Land Use Plan in terms of zoning must be replaced by planning for land as a resource. This implies that Land Use Planning and Urban Planning have to become part of the General Planning Process. Spatial planning, which deals with the use and development of land has to be integrated with economic planning which aims at generating economic growth, and social planning whose concern is social justice and equity.

Such an approach calls for a change in the methodology of planning. Master Planning must be replaced by Metropolitan Planning in a regional dimension. The resources of the entire region would have to be taken into account in formulating the plan. This would include land resources apart from the economic resources. The plan must then look at the socio-economic situation of the region and the needs of the people in terms of employment, shelter, transportation, social facilities and a desirable environment. The major functions of the city—economic and social, must be identified and strategies devised to encourage functions which will promote desirable growth in the region and discourage or deflect functions which are not desirable. Land Use Planning must form part of this broad strategy and land policies must be integrated with the policies for the economic and social development of the region. Hence the need for an integrated land policy.

The first step in formulating an integrated Urban Land Policy is to identify the critical issues pertaining to the region. For the Bangalore metropolitan region, the following issues are crucial:

(i) Rapid growth in population resulting in an increase in demand for land.
(ii) Expanding urban sprawl leading to unplanned developments in rural-urban fringe and higher costs in providing services.

(iii) Very high land prices placing a heavy strain on people's ability to pay for shelter, especially the weaker sections.

The identification of issues must be followed up by determination of objectives. For Bangalore Metropolitan Area, the following objectives would be relevant :

(i) to deflect the growth of Bangalore to other urban centres in the region and the State, and thus reduce the demand for land;
(ii) to contain the expanding urban sprawl within manageable limits;
(iii) to provide land for the major city functions with a bias towards the needs of the low income sections; and
(iv) to control the rising land prices.

The strategies to achieve the above objectives would be :

1. In order to deflect growth from Bangalore, the other cities in the State with growth potential must be identified and provided with adequate infrastructural facilities to attract investments. The policy adopted so far has been half hearted. If other urban centres can generate jobs, people will tend to move to those places. Towns like Ramanagaram, Channapatna and Chikkaballapur in the Bangalore metropolitan region and cities like Mysore, Mangalore and Hubli-Dharwad in the State can become centres to provide such employment.
2. Containment of urban sprawl can be achieved by a two-fold strategy. First, BDA must stop acquiring vast extents of agricultural land which will push the periphery of the city beyond specified limits, especially the green belt. Secondly, specific measures must be taken to promote efficient and economical utilisation of land. All the developed vacant land—public and private, must first be identified and put to use. Preparing an inventory of developed and undeveloped vacant land would help in arriving at a proper estimate of land availability in Bangalore. Thirdly, density standards must be revised to provide for intensive development and better utilisation of space.
3. Supply of land must be oriented towards desirable functions of the city. The policy of allocating land at cheap prices for

unproductive purposes in the metropolitan area must be given up. The needs of the informal sector must be taken into consideration. Supply of publicly acquired land for shelter must be related to promoting economical utilisation of space and low cost housing. Land acquisition must be limited to the minimum quantity required and alternative methods to augment the supply of land like renewal of old central areas, recycling of deteriorating building stock and utilisation of developed vacant land must be explored to meet the requirements of urban growth. Fiscal measures must be oriented towards encouraging the desirable use of land and curbing undesirable use, in keeping with the goals of public policy. Land Policies in India have paid little attention to the demand side of land and concentrated more on the supply side. Only a policy aimed at restraining the demand for land while attempting to augment the supply to meet the growing needs can have a salutary effect on the market and help in controlling land prices.

In view of the intracting instruments that influence the allocation and use of land, no single objective or measure can be viewed in isolation and policy can not be based on any one element. The purpose of an integrated Urban Land Policy is to coordinate the various policy measures—Land Use Planning, taxation and public intervention in the land market — into a single framework to achieve the policy objectives. An integrated approach also calls for an effective apex organisation at the metropolitan level to plan, coordinate and oversee the implementation of policy measures. In respect of Bangalore, the Bangalore Metropolitan Region Development Authority must be strengthened to pay this role.

NOTE

1. Examples are land given for construction of marriage halls and expensive nursing homes which benefit the rich.

BIBLIOGRAPHY

Acharya, B.P., (1988), "The Instruments of Urban Land Policy in India: Opportunities for future direction", *Environment and Planning A*, 1988, Vol. 20: 1427-47.

Alonso, W., (1964), *Location and land use,* Cambridge, Mass.

Archer, R.W., (1974), "The leasehold system of urban development: Land tenure, decision making and the land market in urban development and land use", *Regional Studies 8,* 225-38.

Arora, S., (1982), *Land for Low Income Housing under the Land Banking Programme in Delhi,* unpublished Masters Thesis, Human Settlements Development Division, Asian Institute of Technology, Bangkok.

Bangalore Development Authority, (1984), *Comprehensive Development Plan,* Bangalore Development Authority, Bangalore.

Bails, D., (1974), "Two Municipal Revenue Sources contrasted: The Land Value Tax and the Property Tax", *American Journal of Economics and Sociology,* Vol. 33, No. 2, April 1974.

Bawa, V.K.,(1987), *Indian Metropolis: Urbanisation, Planning and Management,* Inter-India Publication, New Delhi.

Bhargava, G., (1981), *Urban Problems and Policy Perspectives,* Abhinav Publications, New Delhi.

Bijlani, H.U., (1981), *Human Settlement Planning in India,* Economic and Social Commission for Asia and the Pacific, Bangkok.

Branch, M.C., (1975), *Urban Planning Theory,* Dowden, Hutchinson & Ross Fuc, Pennsylvania.

Bose, A., (1978), *India's Urbanization, 1901-2001,* Tata McGraw-Hill Publishing Co. Ltd., New Delhi.

Buch, M.N., (1984), "Land Policy and the Urban Poor", *Nagarlok* 16(4): 1-10.

Burgess; E.W., (1925), The growth of the city: An introduction to a research project, in Park R E and Burgess, E.W., eds (1925): *The City*, 62 Chicago University Press.

Butler, E.W., Chapin, F.S., *et al,* (1969), "Moving behaviour and residential choice: A national survey", *in National Co-operative Highway*

Research Report, 81 U.S. Highway Research Board, Washington D.C.

Carter, H., (1972), *The Study of Urban Geography,* Edward Arnald (Publishers) Ltd., London.

Census of India, 1951, 1961, 1971 and 1981 — Karanataka Series.

Census of India, (1981), Bangalore District Census Handbook, Series-9, Karnataka, Parts XIII - A & B.

Chapin, F.S., (1965), *Urban Land Use Planning,* University of Illinois Press, Chicago.

Clarke, P.N., (1965), "Site Value Rating and the Recovery of Betterment", Peter Hall (ed), *Land Values,* London: 73.

Clawson, M and C. L. Stewart, (1965), *Land Use Information—A Critical Survey of U.S. Statistics,* John Hopkins Press, Baltimore.

Corporation of the City of Bangalore, (1983), *Building Bye Laws — 1983,* Corporation of the City of Bangalore, Bangalore.

Darin-Drabkin, (1977), *Land Policy and Urban Growth,* Pergamon Press, Oxford, England.

Datta, A., (Ed), (1983), *Property Taxation in India,* Centre for Urban Studies, Indian Institute of Public Administration, New Delhi.

David, D.E., *et al.*, (1977), *Land Use Control - Evaluating Economic and Political Effects,* Balbriger Publishing Company, Cambridge, Massachusetts.

Dietrich, G., (1986), "Housing the Urban Poor", *Economic and Political Weekly,* Vol. 21, No. 9, March 1, 1986: 376-79.

Duncan, O.D. and Duncan B (1955), "Residential distribution and occupational stratification", *American Journal of Sociology* 60: 493-503.

Duncan, B., (1964), Variables in Urban Morphology, Burgess E W & Bogue D J ed. (1964), *Contributions to Urban Sociology,* 17 Chicago.

Dutta, S.S., (1964), "Land policies in human settlements: a review of current practices in India", mimeograph, Town & Country Planning Orgn., Govt. of India. New Delhi.

Evans, A.W., (1983), "Determination of the Price of Land", *Urban Studies,* 20(2), May 1983: 119-29.

Firey, W., (1945), Sentiment and Symbolism as ecological variables, *American Sociological Review*: 10, 140.

Form, W.H., (1954), The place of social sturcture in the determination of land use: some implications for a theory of urban ecology, *Social Forces*: 32: 317.

Gallion, A.B., and Ecsner, S., (1984), *The Urban Pattern : City Planning and Design,* C B S Publishers, Delhi.

Gandhi, N. K., (1973), *Study of Town and Country Planning in India,* Indian Town & Country Planning Association, Bombay.

Geddes, P., (1951), *Cities in Evolution,* London, 1915.

Gist, N.P., (1957), The Ecology of Bangalore: An East-West Comparison'', *Social Forces,* Vol 35: pp. 356-65.

Gittus, E.,(1964), The structure of urban areas, A new approach, *Town Planning Review:* 35, 7.

Golledge, R.G., (1960), ''Sydney's metropolitan fringes: a study in urban-rural relations," *Australian Geography:* 7, 243-55.

Government of India, (1965), *Report of the Committee on Urban Land Policy; Ministry of Health, New Delhi.*

—Five Years Plans (I to VII), Planning Commission, New Delhi.

—(1983), *Task Force on Housing and Urban Development on Planning of Urban Development.* Planning Commission, Government of India, New Delhi.

—(1988), *National Housing Policy,* Ministry of Urban Development, New Delhi.

—(1988), *Report of the National Commission on Urbanisation,* Government of India, New Delhi.

Government of Karnataka, Five Year Plans (IV to VII). Planning Department, Government of Karnataka, Bangalore.

—"Land Acquisition", Guidelines issued between 1963 and 1980, Revenue Department, Government of Karnataka, Bangalore.

—"Incentives and Concessions for New Industrial Investments in Karnataka" — Government Orders issued in 1969, 1971, 1980, 1982 Commerce and Industries Department, Government of Karnataka, Bangalore.

—(1968), The Outline Development Plan for the Bangalore Metropolitan Region, Government Press, Bangalore.

—(1972), Outline Development Plan of Bangalore, Government Press, Bangalore.

Government of Karnataka—(1984), Background Paper on Urban Policy in Karnataka, Housing and Urban Development Department, Government of Karnataka, Bangalore.

—(1985), Report of Local Finance Commission on Urban Local Bodies in Karnataka State, Government of Karnataka, Bangalore.

—(1990), *Karnataka State Gazetteer:* Bangalore District, Government of Karnataka, Bangalore.

Grimes, C.F., (1975), Urban Land and Public Policy: Social appropriation of Betterment, World Bank Staff Working Paper No.179, Washington D.C.

Gyanchand, (1947), *Local Finance in India,* Kitabistan, Allahabad.

Haig, R.M., (1926), "Toward an understanding of the metropolis", *Quarterly Journal of Economics*: 40, 421.

Hamilton, F.E.I., (1967), "Models of industrial location", in Chorley, R.J. & Haggett, P., ed (1967): *Models in Geography:* 361 - 417 Mathuen Ltd., London.

Harris, C.D & Ulman, E.L., (1945), "The nature of cities", *Annual American Academy of Political Science*: 242, 7.

Hasan, M.F., (1970), *Bangalore Through the Centuries,* Historical Publications, Bangalore.

Howard, E., (1898), *Garden Cities of Tomorrow,* London.

Howland, M., (1975), "Delhi's Large Scale Land Acquisition. Development and Disposal Policy: An appraisal" *Urban and Rural Planning Thought,* 18(91): 23-54.

Hoyt, H., (1939), *The Structure and growth of residential neighbourhoods in American Cities,* Washington.

Hurd, R.M., (1924), *Principles of city land values,* New York.

Indian Institute of Public Administration, (1977), City Development Plans and their implementation, Centre for Urban Studies, I.I.P.A. New Delhi.

Indian Space Research Organisation, (1985), *Growth of Bangalore City Since 1900 Based on Maps and Satellite Imagery,* Indian Space Research Organisation, Bangalore.

Jha, G., (1983), "Land nationalisation in Delhi: A policy Analysis", *Nagarlok* 15 (2): 9-26.

Johnson, R.J., (1966), "The location of high status residential areas", *Geographic Annaler*, 48B, 25, Stockholm.

Kapoor, R.M., (1977), "Finance of Calcutta Corporation: Problems and Prospects", *Nagarlok,* Vol IX, No. 1, Jan - Mar 1977.

Lichfield, N., (1956), *Economics of Planned Development,* Estates Gazette, London.

Linn, J.F., (1983), *Cities in the Developing World: Policies for their equitable and efficient growth,* World Bank, Oxford University Press, New York.

Lowenstein, L.K., (1963), "The location of urban land uses", *London Economics,* 39, 406-20.

Mahadev, P.D. and P. Boregowda, (1981), Co-operative Sector and Housing Development—A strategy for meeting the Housing Shortage in Bangalore City, Paper presented at Round Table Professional Meet on "Problems of Bangalore and Strategy for Future Development", sponsored by Institute of Town Planners, India.

Marshall, A., (1916), *Principles of Economics,* Macmillan, London.

Mayer, H. (1967), "A Survey of Urban Geography", in Hauser, P. M. & Schnore, L.F. ed (1967) : *The Study of Urbanisation,* John Wily and Sons, New York.

McLoughlin, J.B. (1973), *Control and Urban Planning,* Faber and Faber Ltd., London.

Ministry of Housing and Local Government, (1956), Report of the Ministry for the year 1955, H.M.S.O. London.

Misra, B., (1985), "nstruments of Urban Land Policy" in N.S. Saini and Mahavir (eds.) *Urban Development Planning Strategies and Techniques,* School of Planning and Architecture, New Delhi.

Misra, B., (1986), *Urban Development Policies in India: Focus on Land Management,* Ed. H. Nagamine, U.N. Centre for Regional Development, Nagoya: pp 1-65.

Misra, R.P., (1978), *Million Cities of India,* Vikas Publishing House, New Delhi.

Modak, N.V. and V.N., Ambedkar, *Town and Country Planning and Housing,* Orient Longman Ltd., Bombay.

Mohan, R., (1983), "Indian Thinking on Property Tax Reform" in A. Dutta (ed.) *Property Taxation in India,* Indian Institute of Public Administration, New Delhi.

Moriarty, B.M., (1970), "A test of alternative hypothesis of urban residential growth", *Prov. Assn. of American Geography:* 2, 97-101.

Mukharji, G., (1968), "Urban Land Policy", *The Indian Journal of Public Administration,* Vol. XIV. No. 3, July-Sept, 1968: 582- 95.

Murphy, R.E., and Vance, J.E., (1954), "Delimiting the C B D" *Economic Geography*: 30, 189-222.

National Council of Applied Economic Research, (1980), *A Study of Resources of Municipal Bodies.* NCAER, New Delhi.

Netzer, D., (1966), *Economics of the Property Tax,* Washington D C, The Brookings Institutions, 1966.

Neutze, G.M., (1970 The Price of Land for Economic Development, *Economic Record* 46 (115), World Bank.

Northam, R.M., (1975), *Urban Geography,* John Wiley & Sons, New York.

Pahl, RE., (1965), Urbs in rure, The metropolitan fringe in Hertfordshire, London School of Economics and Political Science, *Geog. Paper 2.*

Patterson, T. W., (1979), *Land Use Planning—Techniques of Implementation,* Van Nastrand Reinhold Company, New York.

Petersen, G.L., (1967), "A model of Preference : quantitative analysis of the perception of visual appearance of residential neighbourhoods", *Journal of Regional Science Assn.* 7, 19-31.

Prakash Rao, V.L.S, and V.K. Tewari, (1978), *Urbanisation in India: Spatial Dimensions,* Institute for Social and Economic Change, Bangalore.

—(1979), *The Structure of an Indian Metropolis : A Study of Bangalore,* Allied Publishers, New Delhi.

Prakash Rao, V.L.S., (1981), "Green Belting the City", Mimeographed, Indian Institute of Management, Bangalore.

—(1983), *Urbanisation in India:Spatial Dimensions,* Concept Publishing Company, New Delhi.

Pred, A.R., (1964), "The intra-metropolitan location of American manufacturing", *Annual Association of American Geography.* 54, 165-80.

Prest, A.R., (1981), *The Taxation of Urban Land,* Manchester University Press, 1981.

Preston, R.E., and Griffin, D.W. (1966), "A restatement of the transition zone concept", *Annual Assn. of American Geogrpahy:* 56, 339-50.

Quinn, J.A., (1939), "The nature of human ecology: re- examination and re-definition", *Social forces:* 18, 166.

Ramakrishna, G.V., (1980), ''Municipal Property Tax: A New Approach'', *Nagarlok,* Vol. XII No. 3, July-Sep 1980.

Rame Gowda, K.S., (1986), *Urban and Regional Planning,* Prasaranga, University of Mysore, Mysore.

Ratcliff, (1949), *Urban land economies,* 369 New York.

Ribeiro, E.F.N., (1982), Urban Land Policies in the context of the Development Plan for Delhi, Paper presented at the Seminar on 'Land in Metropolitan Development, Calcutta, Times Research Foundation, Calcutta'.

Rivkin, M. D., (1983), "Intervention through Direct Participation" in *Urban Land Policy: Issues and Opportunities,* ed. Dunkerley H. B, World Bank.

Schnore, L. F., (1965), "On the spatial structure of cities in the two Americas", in Hauser P M & Schnore L G, ed (1965): *The Study of urbanization;* 353-54, Joh Wiley and Sons, New York.

Schroeder, L., (1980), Property tax assessment problems in the United States and India: some contrasts and comparisons. *Nagarlok* 12:1, Jan-Mar 1980; 1-15.

Shevky, E. and Bell, W., (1955), *Social area analysis;* theory, illustrative application and computational procedure, Stanford University Press.

Shoup, D.C., (1983), "Intervention through Property Taxation and Public Ownership", in *Urban Land Policy: Issues and Opportunities,* ed. Dunkerley HB., World Bank.

Shoup, D.C., and Mack, R.P., (1968), *Advance Land Acquisition by Local Govts,* Washington D.C., U.S. Govt. Printing Office.

Tewari, V.K., (1978), "A Model of Bangalore Metropolis," *Mimeographed,* Institute for Social and Economic Change, Bangalore.

Tewari, V.K., Weinstein, J & V.L.S. Prakasa Rao, (1986), *Indian Cities-Ecological Perspectives,* Concept Publishing Co., New Delhi.

Thomas, D., (1976), "Britain's Green Belts : A Retrospect," *Golden Jubilee Volume, Indian Geographical Society,* Madras, 1976: 65-75.

Town and Country Planning Organisation, (1988), The Management of Urban Fringe Land Development in Bangalore (unpublished Report) TCPO, New Delhi.

United Nations, (1973), *Urban Land Policies and Land Use Control Measures, Vo.II.* Asia and the Far East, United Nations Publications, New York.

—(1977), *Land for Human Settlements,* United Nations, New York.

—(1987), *The Prospects of World Urbanization raised as of 1984-85,* United Nations New York.

Ursula, Hicks, (1961), *Development from Below: Local Govt. and Finance in Commonwealth Countries,* Oxford, Clarendon Press, 1961.

—(1967), *Public Finance,* London, Cambridge University Press 1967.

Venkatarayappa, K. N., (1957), *Bangalore: A Socio-Ecological Study,* University of Bombay, Bombay

Wheeler, JO., (1968), Residential location by occupational status, *Urban Studies* 5, 24.

Wishwakarma, R.K., (1981), *Urban and Regional Planning Policy in India,* Uppal Publishing House, New Delhi

World Bank, (1972), *Urbanization Sector Working Paper,* World Bank, Washington.

—(1978), *Urban Land Policy Issues and Opportunities, Staff Working Paper,* Vol I & II, World Bank, Washington.

—(1983), *Urban Land Policy—Issues and Opportunities,* Ed. Dunkerley H B, World Bank, Washington.

—(1986), India: urban land management study, *unpublished draft report.* World Bank, Washington D C.

All Acts referred to in this book are printed at Government Press, Bangalore.

INDEX